Integrated

Practice
Workbook

Houghton Mifflin Harcourt

ISBN   978-0-544-716537
2 3 4 5 6 7 8 9 10   0982   24 23 22 21 20 19 18
4500705619   A B C D E F G

Contents

Student Worksheets

| LESSON | **Proving Lines Are Parallel** |
| 1-1 | *Practice and Problem Solving: A/B* |

Use the figure for Problems 1–8. Tell whether lines *m* and *n* must be parallel from the given information. If they are, state your reasoning. (*Hint:* The angle measures may change for each problem, and the figure is for reference only.)

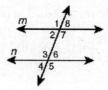

1. $\angle 7 \cong \angle 3$

2. $m\angle 3 = (15x + 22)°$, $m\angle 1 = (19x - 10)°$, $x = 8$

_____

3. $\angle 7 \cong \angle 6$

4. $m\angle 2 = (5x + 3)°$, $m\angle 3 = (8x - 5)°$, $x = 14$

_____

5. $m\angle 8 = (6x - 1)°$, $m\angle 4 = (5x + 3)°$, $x = 9$

6. $\angle 5 \cong \angle 7$

_____

7. $\angle 1 \cong \angle 5$

8. $m\angle 6 = (x + 10)°$, $m\angle 2 = (x + 15)°$

_____

9. Look at some of the printed letters in a textbook. The small horizontal and vertical segments attached to the ends of the letters are called *serifs*. Most of the letters in a textbook are in a serif typeface. The letters on this page do not have serifs, so these letters are in a sans-serif typeface. (*Sans* means "without" in French.) The figure shows a capital letter *A* with serifs. Use the given information to write a paragraph proof that the serif, segment $\overline{HI}$, is parallel to segment $\overline{JK}$.

Given: $\angle 1$ and $\angle 3$ are supplementary.

Prove: $\overline{HI} \parallel \overline{JK}$

Name _____ Date _____ Class_____

LESSON 1-1

Proving Lines Are Parallel

Practice and Problem Solving: C

1. $p \parallel q$, $m\angle 1 = (6x + y - 4)°$, $m\angle 2 = (x - 9y + 1)°$, $m\angle 3 = (11x + 2)°$
   Find x, y, and the measures of $\angle 1$, $\angle 2$, and $\angle 3$.

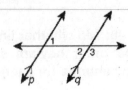

_____

2. A definition of parallel lines is "two coplanar lines that never intersect."
   Imagine railroad tracks or the strings on a guitar. Another way to think
   about parallel lines is that they extend in exactly the same direction.
   Or to say it more mathematically, if a third line intersects one line in a
   right angle and intersects a second line in a right angle, then the first
   and second lines are parallel. Use this last definition as the final step in
   a paragraph proof of the following.

   Given: The sum of the angle measures in any
   triangle is 180°; $\angle 1 \cong \angle 2$

   Prove: $\overleftrightarrow{AB}$ and $\overleftrightarrow{CD}$ are parallel lines.

   (*Hint*: First draw line $\overleftrightarrow{AE}$ so it forms a 90° angle with $\overline{AB}$.
   This step can be justified by the Protractor Postulate.
   On the figure, label the intersection of $\overleftrightarrow{AE}$ and $\overleftrightarrow{CD}$ point F.)

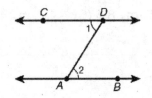

_____

_____

_____

_____

_____

_____

_____

_____

_____

3. $s \parallel t$, $m\angle 1 = (3x - 6)°$, $m\angle 2 = (5x + 2y)°$,
   $m\angle 3 = (x + y + 6)°$; Find x, y, and the measures
   of $\angle 1$, $\angle 2$, and $\angle 3$.

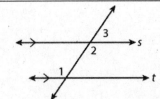

_____

_____

LESSON 1-2

Perpendicular Lines

Practice and Problem Solving: A/B

For Problems 1–2, determine the unknown values.

1. Given: $\overrightarrow{AC}$ is the perpendicular
   bisector of $\overline{GH}$.

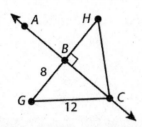

   GH = _____

   CH = _____

2. Given: $\overrightarrow{CD}$ is the perpendicular
   bisector of $\overline{PR}$.

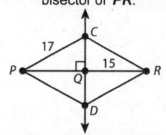

   CR = _____

   PQ = _____

Complete the two-column proof.

3. **Given:** $m \perp n$

   Prove: $\angle 1$ and $\angle 2$ are a linear pair of congruent angles.

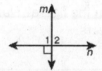

   Proof:

Statements	Reasons
1. a. _____	1. Given
2. b. _____	2. Def. of $\perp$
3. $\angle 1 \cong \angle 2$	3. c. _____
4. $m\angle 1 + m\angle 2 = 180°$	4. Add. Prop. of =
5. d. _____	5. Def. of linear pair

4. The Four Corners National Monument is at the intersection of the
borders of Arizona, Colorado, New Mexico, and Utah. It is called the
four corners because the intersecting borders are perpendicular. If you
were to lie down on the intersection, you could be in four states at the
same time—the only place in the United States where this is possible.
The figure shows the Colorado–Utah border extending north in a
straight line until it intersects the Wyoming border at a right angle.
Explain why the Colorado–Wyoming border must be parallel to the
Colorado–New Mexico border.

_____

_____

_____

LESSON
1-2

Perpendicular Lines

Practice and Problem Solving: C

1. Draw a segment a little more than half the width of this page. Label this segment with length x, then use a compass and straightedge to construct a segment that has length $\frac{5}{4}x$.

2. Among segments $\overline{BA}$, $\overline{BC}$, $\overline{BD}$, and $\overline{BE}$, which is the shortest segment in the figure? Name the second-shortest segment. Explain your answers.

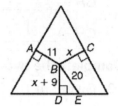

_____

_____

_____

_____

3. Use a straightedge to draw a triangle. Construct the perpendicular bisector of each side of the triangle, and extend the bisectors into the interior of the triangle. Mark the point of intersection of the three bisectors. This is the *circumcenter* of the triangle. Use your compass to compare the distance from the circumcenter to each vertex of the triangle. What is remarkable about the distances?

_____

Now construct a circle completely around the triangle through all three vertices with your compass. You have *circumscribed* a circle around a triangle.

4. An architect designs a triangular jogging track around a circular pond. Each side of the track just touches the pond. The circle is *inscribed* in the triangle. The center of the circle is called the *incenter* of the triangle. The diameter of the circle has length 41.

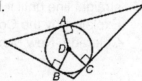

$DA = 8x + 2z - 1\frac{1}{2}$, $DB = 6x + y + 1$, $DC = 11y - 2z + 2$.

Find x, y, and z.

Name _____ Date _____ Class_____

Justifying Constructions
Practice and Problem Solving: A/B

The figure shows the construction line and arcs for drawing the angle bisector of ∠ABC.

1. Name a point on the construction that is the same distance from *D* as *A* is.

   _____

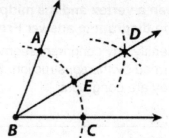

2. Name a line segment that is congruent to $\overline{AB}$.

   _____

3. Suppose you drew segments $\overline{AD}$ and $\overline{DC}$. Which angle congruence theorem could you use to prove that $\triangle BAD \cong \triangle BCD$? Explain your reasoning.

   _____

   _____

   _____

***T* is in the interior of ∠PQR. A student constructs $\overrightarrow{QT}$ so that it bisects ∠PQR. Find each of the following.**

4. m∠PQR if m∠RQT = 11° _____

5. m∠PQR if m∠RQT = (5x − 7)° and m∠PQT = (4x + 6)° _____

6. m∠TQR if m∠RQT = (10x − 13)° and m∠PQT = (6x + 1)° _____

The figure shows △FGH, an isosceles triangle, constructed so that $GH = FH$ and $\overline{GL}$ and $\overline{FL}$ are angle bisectors. Find each of the following quantities.

7. m∠FGL = _____

8. m∠GFL = _____

9. m∠GLF = _____

10. Joseph constructed two parallel lines and labeled the angles formed so that ∠3 and ∠7 were corresponding. He labeled m∠3 as (5x + 3)° and m∠7 as 68°. What is the value of *x*?

   _____

LESSON
1-3
Justifying Constructions
Practice and Problem Solving: C

The diagram below shows how to construct one of the
medians of the triangle. A median is a line segment
between a vertex and the midpoint of the opposite side.
Use the diagram to answer Problem 1.

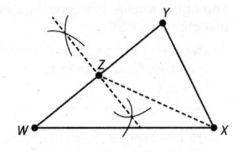

1. Identify any congruent segments and angles
   formed by the construction. Explain how you know
   they are congruent.

   _____

   _____

   _____

2. The figure at the right shows the result if the construction
   is completed and the midpoints are connected. Describe
   three pairs of congruent angles in the figure. Then identify
   the theorem that proves that they are congruent.

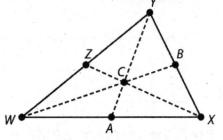

   _____

   _____

   _____

3. In an isosceles triangle, at least two of the angles are congruent. To
   construct isosceles triangle *DEH*, begin by drawing $\overline{DE}$ and $\overline{DF}$. If
   you copy ∠*FDE* and let the angle open in the same direction, the ray
   would be parallel to $\overrightarrow{DF}$. Instead, copy ∠*FDE* and draw $\overrightarrow{EG}$ so that
   the ray intersects $\overline{DF}$. Label the intersection point *H*. Measure $\overline{DH}$
   and $\overline{EH}$. What is remarkable about the lengths of these segments?

   _____

   _____

   _____

   _____

Name _____ Date _____ Class_____

Properties of Parallelograms
Practice and Problem Solving: A/B

PQRS is a parallelogram. Find each measure.

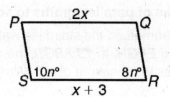

1. *RS* _____

2. m∠*S* _____

3. m∠*R* _____

The figure shows a swing blown to one side by a
breeze. As long as the seat of the swing is parallel to
the top bar, the swing makes a parallelogram. In

▱ *ABCD*, *DC* = 2 ft, *BE* = $4\frac{1}{2}$ ft, and m∠*BAD* = 75°.

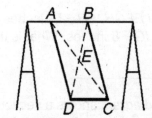

Find each measure.

4. *AB* _____   5. *ED* _____   6. *BD* _____

7. m∠*ABC* _____   8. m∠*BCD* _____   9. m∠*ADC* _____

**Three vertices of ▱ *GHIJ* are *G*(0, 0), *H*(2, 3), and *J*(6, 1).
Use the grid to the right to complete Problems 10–16.**

10. Plot vertices *G*, *H*, and *J* on the coordinate plane.

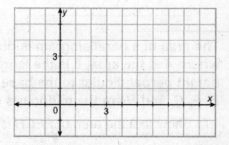

11. Find the rise (difference in the *y*-coordinates) from

   G to *H*. _____

12. Find the run (difference in the *x*-coordinates) from

   G to *H*. _____

13. Using your answers from Problems 11 and 12, add the rise to the
    y-coordinate of vertex *J* and add the run to the *x*-coordinate of vertex *J*.
    The coordinates of vertex *I* are (_____, _____).

14. Plot vertex *I*. Connect the points to draw ▱ *GHIJ*.

15. Check your answer by finding the slopes of $\overline{IH}$ and $\overline{JG}$.

   slope of $\overline{IH}$ = _____   slope of $\overline{JG}$ = _____

16. What do the slopes tell you about $\overline{IH}$ and $\overline{JG}$? _____

_____

LESSON 1-4

Properties of Parallelograms

Practice and Problem Solving: C

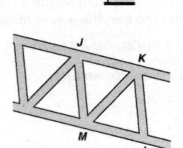

Use properties of parallelograms to solve Problems 1–3.

1. The wall frames on the staircase wall form parallelograms *ABCD* and *EFGH*. In ▱ *ABCD*, the measure of ∠*A* is three times the measure of ∠*B*. What are the measures

   of ∠*C* and ∠*D*? _____; _____

2. In ▱ *EFGH*, *FH* = 5*x* inches, *EG* = (2*x* + 4) inches, and *JG* = 8 inches. What is the length of *JH*?

   _____

3. The diagram shows a section of the support structure of a roller coaster. In ▱ *JKLM*, *JK* = (3*z* − 0.9) feet and

   LM = (*z* + 2.7) feet. Find *JK*. _____

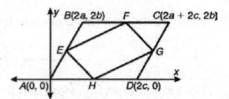

Find the range of possible diagonal lengths in a parallelogram with the given side lengths.

4. 3 and 12

5. *x* and 2*x*

6. *x* and *x*

   _____   _____   _____

The area of a parallelogram is given by the formula *A* = *bh*, where *A* is the area, *b* is the length of a base, and *h* is the height perpendicular to the base. *ABCD* is a parallelogram. *E*, *F*, *G*, and *H* are the midpoints of the sides.

[Graph: y-axis, B(2a, 2b), F, C(2a + 2c, 2b); E, G; A(0, 0), H, D(2c, 0), x-axis]

7. Show that the area of *EFGH* is half the area of *ABCD*.

8. Show that *EFGH* is a parallelogram.

Name _____ Date _____ Class _____

Slope and Parallel Lines

Practice and Problem Solving: A/B

Line *A* contains the points (2, 6) and (4, 10). Line *B* contains the points (−2, 3) and (3, 13).

1. Are the lines parallel? Explain your reasoning.

_____

_____

Figure *JKLM* has as its vertices the points *J*(4, 4), *K*(2, 1), *L*(−3, 2), and *M*(−1, 5).

Find each slope.

2. $\overline{JK}$ 3. $\overline{KL}$ 4. $\overline{LM}$ 5. $\overline{MJ}$

_____   _____   _____   _____

6. Is *JKLM* a parallelogram? Explain your reasoning.

_____

_____

For Problems 7–10, use the graph at the right.

7. Find the slope of line ℓ.

_____

8. Explain how you found the slope.

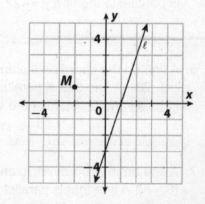

_____

_____

9. Line *m* is parallel to line ℓ and passes through point *M*. Find the slope of line *m*.

_____

10. Find the equation of line *m*. Explain how you found the equation.

_____

_____

_____

Slope and Parallel Lines
Practice and Problem Solving: C

Write the equation of the line that is parallel to the graph of the given equation and that passes through the given point.

1. $y = -6x + 4$; $(-2, 3)$

2. $y = x$; $(7, -2)$

_____   _____

3. Quadrilateral *ABCD* has vertices $A(-1, 5)$, $B(4, 0)$, $C(1, -5)$, and $D(-5, 1)$. Calculate the slopes of the sides, and then use your results to explain whether *ABCD* is or is not a parallelogram.

_____

_____

_____

4. Find the equation of the line parallel to $2x + 5y = 3$ and $2x + 5y = 7$ that lies midway between them.

_____

5. A line that passes through the points $(2, -3)$ and $(b, 7)$ is parallel to the line $y = -2x + 17$. Find the value of *b*.

_____

6. A line on the coordinate plane passes through the points $(-7, 8)$ and $(-7, 20)$. A line that is parallel to the first line passes through the points $(11, -4)$ and $(x, 9)$. Find the value of *x*.

_____

7. A line on the coordinate plane passes through the points $(-3, -7)$ and $(0, -5)$. A line that is parallel to the first line passes through the points $(6, 4)$ and $(-9, y)$. Find the value of *y*.

_____

8. Line *L* has the equation $ax + by = c$. Line *M* is parallel to Line *L*. What is the slope of Line *M*?

_____

Slope and Perpendicular Lines

LESSON 2-2

Practice and Problem Solving: A/B

Line *A* contains the points (−1, 5) and (1, −3). Line *B* contains the points (2, 3) and (−2, 2).

1. Are the lines perpendicular? Explain your reasoning.

_____

_____

Figure *WXYZ* has as its vertices the points *W*(2, 7), *X*(5, 6), *Y*(5, −4), and *Z*(−1, −2).

Find each slope.

2. $\overline{WX}$ 3. $\overline{XY}$ 4. $\overline{YZ}$ 5. $\overline{ZW}$

_____   _____   _____   _____

6. Is Figure *WXYZ* a rectangle? Explain your reasoning.

_____

_____

For Problems 7–10, use the graph at the right.

7. Find the slope of line ℓ.

_____

8. Explain how you found the slope.

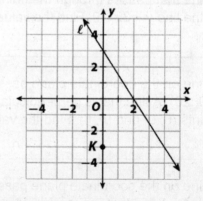

_____

_____

9. Line *t* is perpendicular to line ℓ and passes through point *K*.
   Find the slope of line *t*.

_____

10. Find the equation of line *t*. Explain how you found the equation.

_____

_____

_____

Name _____ Date _____ Class_____

Slope and Perpendicular Lines
Practice and Problem Solving: C

Write the equation of the line that is perpendicular to the graph of the given equation and passes through the given point.

1. $x - 6y = 2$; (2, 4)

2. $y = -3x + 7$; (−3, 1)

_____

_____

For Problems 3–4, write the equation of the line that passes through the point (2, 7) and is perpendicular to the given line.

3. $y = -5$

4. $x = -5$

_____

_____

5. The sidewalks at a park can be modeled by the equations:
$3(y + 1) = 2x$, $2y - 8 = -3x$, $2x + 3 = 3y$, and $-2(y - 12) = 3x$.
Determine the slopes of the equations, and then use them to
classify the quadrilateral bounded by the sidewalks.

_____

_____

6. A line that passes through the points (2, 1) and (k, 5) is perpendicular
to the line $y = 3x - 9$. Find the value of k.

_____

7. A line on the coordinate plane passes through the points (−3, 8) and
(−9, 20). A line that is perpendicular to the first line passes through the
points (5, 0) and (h, 6). Find the value of h.

_____

8. A line on the coordinate plane passes through the points (7, −5) and
(3, 11). A line that is perpendicular to the first line passes through the
points (−3, −9) and (5, n). Find the value of n.

_____

9. The lines $x = 0$, $y = 2x - 5$, and $y = mx + 9$ form a right triangle. Find
two possible values of m.

_____

LESSON 2-3

Coordinate Proof Using Distance with Segments and Triangles
Practice and Problem Solving: A/B

Position an isosceles triangle with sides of 8 units, 5 units, and
5 units in the coordinate plane. Label the coordinates of each vertex.
(*Hint:* Use the Pythagorean Theorem.)

1. Center the long side on the *x*-axis at the origin.

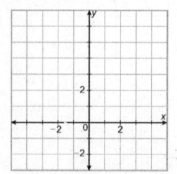

2. Center the long side on the *y*-axis at the origin.

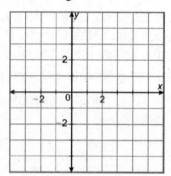

Complete Problems 3–5 to finish the proof.

Given: Triangle *ABC* is an isosceles triangle
with vertices *A*(0, 0), *B*(8, 0), *C*(4, 10). Points
D, E, F are the midpoints of triangle *ABC*.

Prove: Triangle *DEF* is an isosceles triangle.

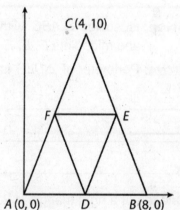

3. Use the midpoint formula to find the coordinates:

   D _____ *E* _____ *F* _____

4. Use the distance formula to show equal side lengths.

   DE = _____ *DF* = _____

5. Suppose, instead, that you want to use △*ABC* to prove
   the Midsegment Theorem, given that $\overline{FE}$ is a midsegment
   and $\overline{AB} \parallel \overline{FE}$. What other steps would you need in the

   coordinate proof? _____

   _____

LESSON 2-3

Coordinate Proof Using Distance with Segments and Triangles

Practice and Problem Solving: C

1. Position an isosceles triangle on the coordinate plane at the right so that you can use it for a coordinate proof. Place its base on the *x*-axis and draw it so that it is symmetric about the *y*-axis. Label the vertices $A(2a, 0)$, $B(0, 2b)$, and $C(-2a, 0)$.

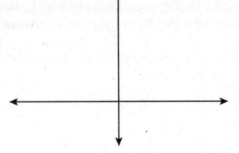

2. Using the vertices given, determine the midpoint of each side of the triangle. Plot the midpoints on the graph. Place the label *D* for side $\overline{AB}$, the label *E* for side $\overline{BC}$, and the label *F* for side $\overline{CA}$. Then draw segments to connect the midpoints.

   Midpoints: *D* _____ *E* _____ *F* _____

3. Use the graph you have constructed to write a coordinate proof.

   Given: Isosceles $\triangle ABC$ with $AB = BC$
   and midpoints *D, E, F*
   Prove: Perimeter of $\triangle DEF$ is one-half the perimeter of $\triangle ABC$.

   _____

   _____

   _____

4. One leg of a right triangle is 2.5 times the length of the other leg. Draw the triangle in the first quadrant of the coordinate plane with the legs along the axes and a vertex at the origin. Use only integer values for your coordinates and write each value as a multiple of *a*.

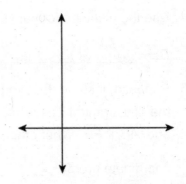

LESSON 2-4

Coordinate Proof Using Distance with Quadrilaterals

Practice and Problem Solving: A/B

Position a trapezoid with parallel sides of 4 units and 6 units in the coordinate plane. Label the coordinates of each vertex.

1. Center the long parallel side at the origin.

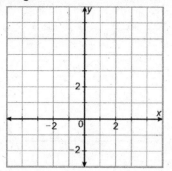

2. Center the long parallel side on the y-axis at the origin.

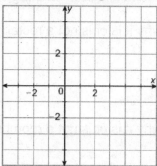

3. Describe the possible steps in a coordinate proof that would show that the figure you drew in Problem 1 is a trapezoid.

_____

_____

_____

Write a coordinate proof.

4. **Given:** Rectangle *ABCD* has vertices *A*(0, 4), *B*(6, 4), *C*(6, 0), and *D*(0, 0). *E* is the midpoint of $\overline{DC}$. *F* is the midpoint of $\overline{DA}$.

   Prove: The area of rectangle *DEGF* is one-fourth the area of rectangle *ABCD*.

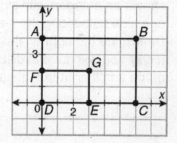

_____

_____

_____

_____

_____

LESSON 2-4

Coordinate Proof Using Distance with Quadrilaterals

Practice and Problem Solving: C

1. A parallelogram has vertices $J(0, -4)$, $K(5, -1)$, $L(4, 4)$, and $M(-1, 1)$.
   Use a coordinate proof to decide whether it is a rectangle, a rhombus,
   or a square. It may be neither, or it may be more than one of these.

   a. Draw the parallelogram on the grid.

   b. Explain why it is or is not a rectangle.

   _____

   _____

   c. Explain why it is or is not a rhombus.

   _____

   _____

   d. Explain why it is or is not a square.

   _____

   _____

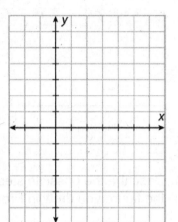

2. A stop sign is a regular octagon. A regular octagon has eight
   congruent sides and eight congruent 135° angles. The figure
   shows an octagon with side length ℓ in a coordinate plane so that
   one side falls along the *x*-axis and one side falls along the *y*-axis.
   Determine the coordinates of each vertex in terms of ℓ.
   (*Hint:* You will have to discover a relationship between the sides
   of the small right triangle at the origin.)

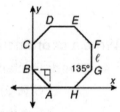

   _____

   _____

3. A "slow down" sign is a regular hexagon. A regular hexagon has
   six congruent sides and six congruent 120° angles. The ℓ figure
   shows a hexagon with side length ℓ in a coordinate plane so that
   one side falls along the *x*-axis and one vertex falls along the *y*-axis.
   Determine the coordinates of each vertex in terms of ℓ.

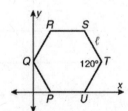

   _____

   _____

Name _____ Date _____ Class_____

Perimeter and Area on the Coordinate Plane

Practice and Problem Solving: A/B

Draw and classify each polygon with the given vertices. Find the perimeter and area of the polygon to the nearest tenth.

1. *A*(–2, 3), *B*(3, 1), *C*(–2, –1), *D*(–3, 1)

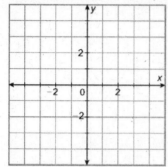

_____

2. *P*(–3, –4), *Q*(3, –3), *R*(3, –2), *S*(–3, 2)

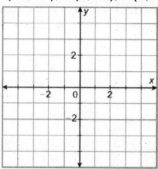

_____

3. *E*(–4, 1), *F*(–2, 3), *G*(–2, –4)

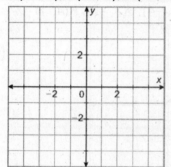

_____

4. *T*(1, –2), *U*(4, 1), *V*(2, 3), *W*(–1, 0)

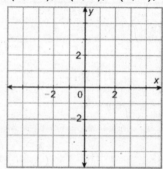

_____

Find the area and perimeter of each composite figure to the nearest tenth.

5.

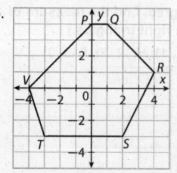

_____

6.

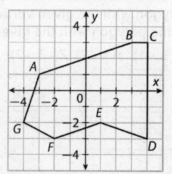

_____

Perimeter and Area on the Coordinate Plane

LESSON 2-5

Practice and Problem Solving: C

Draw each polygon with the given vertices. Find the perimeter and area of the polygon to the nearest tenth.

1. $A(0, 0)$, $B(2, 2)$, $C(-2, 0)$, $D(1, -2)$

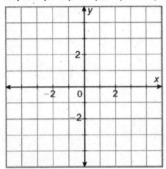

_____

2. $J(2, 4)$, $K(3, -4)$, $L(1, -2)$, $M(-1, -4)$

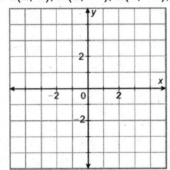

_____

3. $P(-3, 3)$, $Q(1, 2)$, $R(3, -3)$, $S(1, -3)$, $T(-2, -2)$

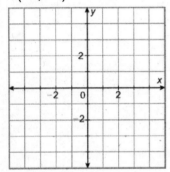

_____

4. $D(2, -1)$, $E(0, 0)$, $F(1, -2)$, $G(0, -4)$, $H(2, -3)$, $I(3, -4)$, $J(3, -2)$, $K(4, 1)$

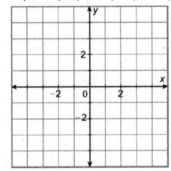

_____

Draw each polygon with the given vertices. To the nearest degree, find the measure of each angle in the polygon with the given vertices. (*Hint:* Form right triangles.)

5. $W(0, 0)$, $X(3, -1)$, $Y(1, -2)$, $Z(-2, -2)$

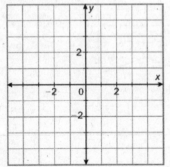

_____

_____

6. $F(3, 4)$, $G(1, 1)$, $H(-2, 2)$, $I(-3, 3)$

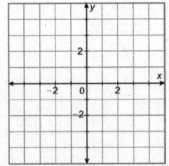

_____

_____

Name _____ Date _____ Class_____

Find the coordinates of point *Q* that subdivides the segment with the given endpoints into two sub-segments with the given ratio. In each case, graph both the segment and the point *Q*.

1. endpoints: *A*(−4, −2), *B*(1, 8)
   ratio: 4 to 1

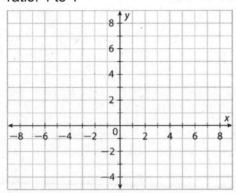

   Q (_____, _____)

2. endpoints: *S*(−6, 6), *T*(6, −2)
   ratio: 1 to 4

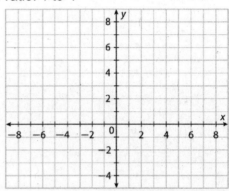

   Q (_____, _____)

3. endpoints: *G*(−3, −4), *Z*(0, 8)
   ratio: 2 to 1

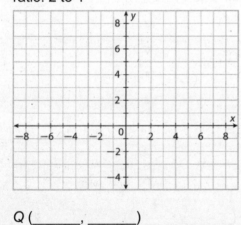

   Q (_____, _____)

4. endpoints: *J*(−7, 2), *K*(8, −3)
   ratio: 2 to 3

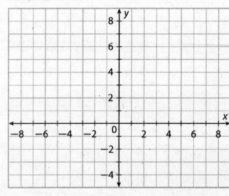

   Q (_____, _____)

Construct the point *P* that divides the segment into two sub-segments with the given ratio.

5. Ratio 2 to 1

6. Ratio 3 to 2

Name _____ Date _____ Class_____

Subdividing a Segment in a Given Ratio
Practice and Problem Solving: C

Find the coordinates of point *Q* that subdivides the segment with the given endpoints into two sub-segments with the given ratio. Round answers to the nearest tenth. Graph both the segment and the point *Q*.

1. endpoints: *A*(–6, 7), *B*(4, –4)
   ratio: 5 to 2

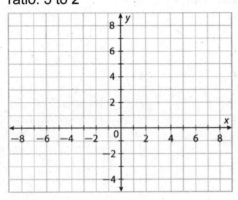

Q (_____, _____)

2. endpoints: *Y*(–6, 2), *Z*(8, 8)
   ratio: 3 to 2

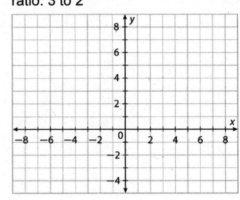

Q (_____, _____)

3. endpoints: *D*(–3, 6), *E*(7, –3)
   ratio: 5 to 3

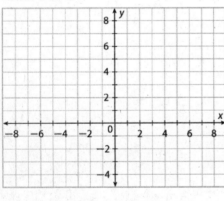

Q (_____, _____)

4. endpoints: *R*(–7, 2), *S*(8, 3)
   ratio: 2 to 7

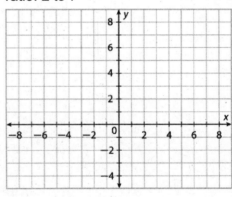

Q (_____, _____)

Construct the point *Q* that divides the segment into two sub-segments with the given ratio.

5. Ratio 3 to 4

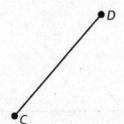

6. Ratio 5 to 1

Name _____ Date _____ Class _____

For Problems 1–6, tell what kind of solid can be made from each net. If there is no solid that can be made from the given net, write "none."

1.

_____

2.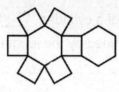

_____

3.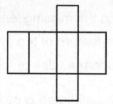

_____

4.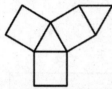

_____

5.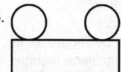

_____

6.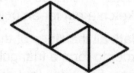

_____

For Problems 7–13, name the shape of the cross section produced by slicing each of these solids as described.

7. Vertical cross section of a cylinder _____

8. Horizontal cross section of a cylinder _____

9. Cross section of a sphere not through the diameter _____

10. Horizontal cross section of a square pyramid _____

11. Vertical cross section of a square pyramid through the top vertex _____

12. Vertical cross section of a square pyramid not through the top vertex _____

13. Horizontal cross section of a rectangular prism _____

14. What can be said about the shape of a cross section that is parallel to the base of a solid? _____

Describe how to generate each 3-dimensional figure by rotating a 2-dimensional figure around a line.

15. Cone _____

16. Sphere _____

17. Cylinder _____

Name _____ Date _____ Class_____

 # Cross Sections and Solids of Rotation
Practice and Problem Solving: C

To solve Problems 1–3, think about how nets can be used to form solid figures.

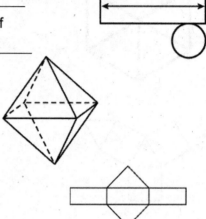

1. Name the missing length for this net of a cylinder. _____

   What feature of the cylinder is determined by the length of

   the shorter sides of the rectangle? _____

2. This solid figure is called a regular octahedron. It is two square pyramids joined at their bases. The faces are all equilateral triangles. Sketch a net for an octahedron.

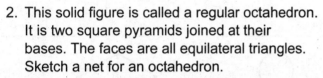

3. Mark all the sides of this net that must be congruent in order to form a triangular prism with a scalene triangle base. For sides that do not *have* to be congruent, use a different number of slash marks.

Think about the properties of 3-dimensional figures to solve Problems 4–10.

4. Name the two possible geometric figures that can result from the

   intersection of a plane and a sphere. _____

5. A square pyramid is intersected by a plane at a 45° angle from horizontal. What shape is the cross section? _____

6. A plane that intersects a cylinder horizontally creates a circular cross section. If the plane intersects the cylinder at an angle, what shape is

   the cross section? _____

7. If a plane intersects a cube at an angle so as to slice off one of its

   corners, what shape is the cross section? _____

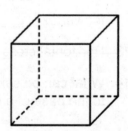

8. If a plane intersects a 1-inch cube at a 45° angle through opposite edges, what are the dimensions of the cross section?

   _____

9. Sketch a plane intersecting the cube to create a hexagon.

10. Sketch a figure that could be rotated around this line to create a torus (donut shape).

LESSON
3-2

Surface Area of Prisms and Cylinders

Practice and Problem Solving: A/B

For Problems 1–6, find the surface area of each solid figure. For Problems 1–4, write the measures of the solid figures on the corresponding parts of their nets. For cylinders, give answers in terms of π.

1. Cube: _____ units²

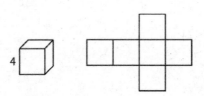

2. Cylinder: _____ units²

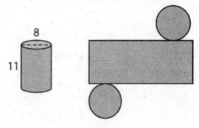

3. Rectangular prism: _____ units²

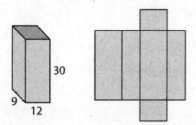

4. Triangular prism: _____ units²

Height of base = 25 units

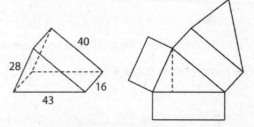

5. Cylinder: _____ units²

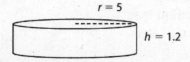

6. Triangular prism: _____ units²

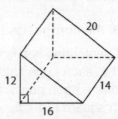

For Problems 7 and 8, find the surface area of each composite figure. Show your work.

7. Cylinder on top of rectangular prism

   _____ units²

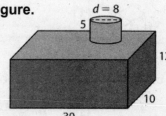

8. 5-inch cube with 2-inch cylinder removed

   _____ units²

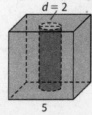

Name _____ Date _____ Class_____

Surface Area of Prisms and Cylinders
Practice and Problem Solving: C

Find the surface area of each figure. Show your work.
For Problems 1–3, sketch a net of the figure.

1. Cylinder whose diameter is

   equal to its height _____ units^2

2. Triangular prism _____ units^2
   (Round lengths to nearest 0.1 units.)

   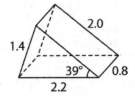

3. Rectangular prism _____ cm^2

   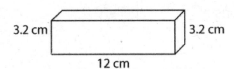

4. The rectangular prism above represents a stick of butter. The

   dimensions in inches are about $1\frac{1}{4} \times 1\frac{1}{4} \times 4\frac{3}{4}$. Find the surface area

   in square inches. _____ in^2

   Multiply your answer by 6.45 to get the
   approximate equivalent in square centimeters. _____ cm^2 .

Find the surface area of the composite shapes.

5. A three-dimensional pentomino is a figure formed by five identical
   cubes arranged so that each cube shares a common face with at least
   one other cube. Visualize each pentomino in 3D and find its surface
   area, given that each square is 1 square unit.

            _____

6. Find the surface area of the cube with a cylinder removed.

   _____ cm^2

   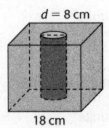

LESSON 3-3

Surface Area of Pyramids and Cones

Practice and Problem Solving: A/B

For Problems 1–4, find the surface area of each part of the solid figure.
Add to find the total surface area. For cones, give answers in terms of π.

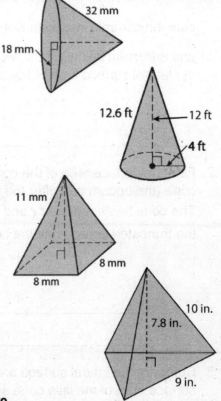

1. What is the base area of the cone?   _____ mm²

   What is the lateral surface area?   _____ mm²

   What is the total surface area?   _____ mm²

2. What is the base area of the cone?   _____ ft²

   What is the lateral surface area?   _____ ft²

   What is the total surface area?   _____ ft²

3. What is the base area of the pyramid?   _____ mm²

   What is the lateral surface area?   _____ mm²

   What is the total surface area?   _____ mm²

4. What is the base area of the pyramid?   _____ in²

   What is the lateral surface area?   _____ in²

   What is the total surface area?   _____ in²

For Problems 5 and 6, find the surface area of each figure.

5. _____ in²

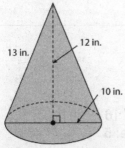

6. _____ cm²

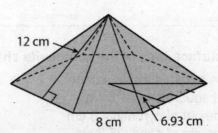

For Problems 7 and 8, find the surface area of each composite figure.

7. _____ m²

8. _____ cm²

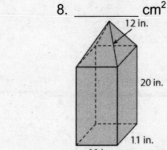

LESSON
3-3

Surface Area of Pyramids and Cones

Practice and Problem Solving: C

Find the surface area of each figure. Show your work.

1. The square pyramid to the right has a base length of *b* and a slant height of ℓ. The gray plane is parallel to the base and cuts the pyramid into a smaller pyramid above with base $\frac{b}{2}$ and a frustum below. Show two different ways to calculate the lateral surface area of the frustum.

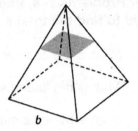

_____

_____

2. Find the surface area of the cone and then of the truncated cone (the bottom part after the top is sliced off by the plane). The cone has a radius of *r* and slant height of ℓ. The height of the truncated cone is half the height of the cone.

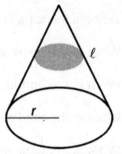

_____

_____

3. Compare the lateral surface area of the big cone with the lateral surface area of the little cone and of the truncated cone.

_____

_____

Find the surface area of the composite shapes. Show your work.

4. Square pyramid inside a cone
   side of square base = 6 cm
   slant height of pyramid = 5 cm
   slant height of cone = 5.8 cm

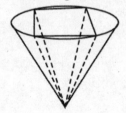

_____

5. Double cone
   radius of base: 12
   height of left cone: 16
   height of right cone: 5

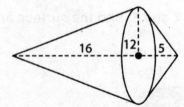

_____

LESSON
3-4

Surface Area of Spheres

Practice and Problem Solving: A/B

Solve Problems 1–8 about the surface area of spheres.
Give surface areas in terms of π.

1. Surface area = _____ mi^2

2. Surface area = _____ m^2

3. What is the total surface area of the hemisphere? _____ in^2
   Show your work.

4. If the radius of the grapefruit is 5 centimeters, what is the surface area

   of the half grapefruit? _____ cm^2 Show your work.

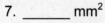

5. If you double the length, width, and height of a rectangular prism, what

   happens to the surface area? _____

   If you double the radius of a sphere, what happens to the surface area?

   _____

   Write equations to prove your answer.

   _____

6. In the case of the prism, you doubled three dimensions. In the
   case of the sphere, you doubled just the radius. Why do you
   get the same results?

   _____

Find the surface area of each composite figure. Show your work.

7. _____ mm^2

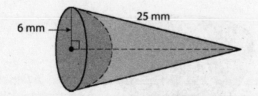

8. _____ in^2

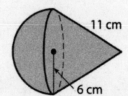

Name _____ Date _____ Class_____

LESSON 3-4
Surface Area of Spheres
Practice and Problem Solving: C

Find the surface areas of the given figures in terms of π. Show your work in the space to the right.

1. The volume of a sphere is given by the formula $V = \frac{4}{3}\pi r^3$. What is the

   surface area of a sphere whose volume is $\frac{256\pi}{3}$ yd^3? _____ yd^2

2. Ganymede, one of Jupiter's moons, is the largest moon in the solar system, with a radius of 1640 miles. The radius of Earth's moon is approximately 1080 miles. Find the surface area of each. About how many times as great is the surface area of Ganymede as the surface area of Earth's moon? Compare the ratio of their surface areas to the ratio of their radii.

   Ganymede: _____ mi^2 Moon: _____ mi^2

   Ratio of surface areas: _____   Ratio of radii: _____

3. What is the surface area of a sphere with a
   great circle whose area is 225π cm^2? _____ cm^2

   Make a general statement about the surface area of a sphere and the area of its great circle.

   _____

4. The three tennis balls just fit in this can with the lid on. Find the surface area of the can and of the three balls in terms of π and the radius r.

   SA of can _____ in^2 *SA* of 3 balls _____ in^2

5. In Problem 4, what do you notice about the surface area of a sphere and the lateral surface area of a cylinder with the same radius?

   _____

Find the surface area of each composite figure. Show your work.

6. _____ in^2

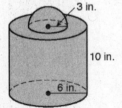

3 in.

10 in.

6 in.

7. _____ ft^2

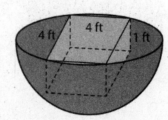

4 ft   4 ft   1 ft

LESSON
4-1

Scale Factor

Practice and Problem Solving: A/B

In Problems 1–3, state how each transformation affects the area.

1. The base of a parallelogram is multiplied by $\frac{3}{4}$.

   _____

2. A rectangle has length 12 yd and width 11 yd. The length is divided by 6.

   _____

3. A triangle has vertices $A(2, 3)$, $B(5, 2)$, and $C(5, 4)$. The transformation is $(x, y) \rightarrow (x, 2y)$.

   _____

In Problems 4–6, state how each transformation affects the perimeter or circumference and area.

4. The length and width of the rectangle are multiplied by $\frac{4}{3}$.

   _____

5. A triangle has base 1.5 m and height 6 m. Both base and height are tripled.

   _____

6. A circle with radius 2 has center (2, 2). The transformation is $(x, y) \rightarrow \left(\frac{1}{2}x, \frac{1}{2}y \right)$.

   _____

In Problems 7 and 8, state how each transformation affects the surface area and volume.

7. The dimensions of a rectangular prism are multiplied by a scale factor of 2.

   _____

8. The dimensions of a right cylinder are multiplied by a scale factor of $\frac{1}{2}$.

   _____

Name _____ Date _____ Class _____

LESSON 4-1 Scale Factor

Practice and Problem Solving: C

Irene has learned how to solve problems about the effects of changing dimensions, but she is suspicious about math formulas until she has seen a proof. Complete Problems 1 and 2 to assuage Irene's doubts. Use A_i to indicate the initial area and A_c to indicate the changed area.

1. Show that multiplying the base and the height of a triangle by n multiplies the area by n^2.

   _____

   _____

   _____

2. Show that multiplying the radius of a circle by n multiplies the area by n^2.

   _____

   _____

   _____

For Problems 3–5, assume the resulting figure is similar to the original. Give answers in simplest radical form.

3. The area of a circle with radius 9 ft is multiplied by $\dfrac{5}{2}$.

   Find the length of the radius of the resulting circle.   _____

4. The area of a square with diagonals $\sqrt{2}$ in. long is doubled.
   Find the length of a side of the resulting square.   _____

5. The area of a circle with a radius of $\sqrt{3}$ cm is squared.
   Find the length of the radius of the resulting circle.   _____

The volume of a rectangular prism can be found with the formula $V = \ell wh$, in which V is the volume, ℓ is the length, w is the width, and h is the height.

6. Describe the effect on the volume of multiplying the height of a rectangular prism by 5.   _____

7. Describe the effect on the volume of multiplying the length, the width, and the height of a rectangular prism by 2.   _____

8. The volume of a rectangular prism is divided by 343 without changing the ratios among the length, width, and height. Describe the effect of the volume change on the height.   _____

Modeling and Density

Practice and Problem Solving: A/B

In Problems 1–3, find the population density.

1. Park rangers counted 7 coyotes over an area of 25 square miles.

   _____

2. A major metropolitan city has an average of 60,000 people visiting the city's park during peak hours. The city park is 3.41 km².

   _____

3. About 50,000 full-grown Canadian geese were estimated to live in the state of Minnesota in 1990. The state of Minnesota is about 86,000 square miles.

   _____

In Problems 4–6, state how the following changes will affect the population density.

4. Park rangers counted 7 coyotes over an area of 25 square miles. One of the coyotes left the pack and is no longer in the area.

   _____

5. A major metropolitan city has an average of 60,000 people visit the city's park during peak hours. The city park is 3.41 km². An outdoor concert is planned in the park and 40,000 additional people are expected to attend the concert.

   _____

6. About 50,000 full-grown Canadian geese were estimated to live in the state of Minnesota in 1990. The state of Minnesota is about 86,000 square miles. It is estimated that 62,000 goslings were produced and will become full-grown adults in 1991.

   _____

Find the population density.

7. Cardton City has a population of 2046. Its border can be modeled by a rectangle with vertices $A(-1, 1)$, $B(1, 1)$, $C(1, 0)$, and $D(-1, 0)$, where each unit on the coordinate plane represents 1 mile. Find the approximate population density of Cardton City.

Modeling and Density

Practice and Problem Solving: C

For Problems 1–4, use the information below to answer the population density questions.

On a range of 250 acres, there was a total of 960 rabbits. During the following year studies indicate the rates for this population:

Birthrate – 2925/yr   Moving into range – 125/yr
Mortality – 1530/yr   Moving out of range – 550/yr

1. What was the population density at the beginning of the study?

   _____

2. Is the population of rabbits increasing or decreasing each year based on the studies?

   _____

3. Calculate the population density at the end of the first year.

   _____

4. A large number of people start setting out traps for the rabbits. What is likely to happen to the population density with this change?

   _____

For Problems 5–8, use the information below to answer the population density questions.

On September 1, 2005, at the beginning of the squirrel-hunting season, biologists counted 85 red squirrels in a 25-acre forest. On December 1, 2005, 32 red squirrels were counted in the forest.

5. What was the density of the red squirrel population on September 1, 2005?

   _____

6. What was the density of the red squirrel population on December 15, 2005?

   _____

7. What factors could have affected the density of the population between September 1, 2005 and December 15, 2005?

   _____

LESSON 4-3

Problem Solving with Constraints

Practice and Problem Solving: A/B

In Problems 1–4, solve for the missing dimension of the figure.

1. A rectangular prism has a volume of 432 cubic feet. Two of the dimensions of the rectangular prism are the same measure. The other dimension is equal to the sum of the other two dimensions. What are the prism's dimensions?

   _____

2. A cone's height is six times greater than the measure of the cone's radius. The volume of the cylinder is 169.56 in^3. What are the cone's dimensions? Use 3.14 for π.

   _____

3. A cube has a volume of 343 cubic centimeters. The length, width, and the height of the figure are equal. What are the cube's dimensions?

   _____

4. A circle has an area of 530.66 square inches. What is the circle's radius? Use 3.14 for π.

   _____

In Problems 5–7, solve the problems using the information provided.

5. The height of a cylindrical can is 2.25 inches greater than the measure of the can's diameter. The volume of the cylinder is 52.18 in^3. What are the can's dimensions? Use 3.14 for π.

   _____

6. A tennis court in the shape of a rectangle has an area of 7200 square feet. One pair of sides measures twice the length of the other pair of sides. What are the dimensions of the tennis court?

   _____

7. A fountain is in the shape of a right triangle. The area of the fountain is 12 square meters. One leg of the triangle measures one and a half times the length of the other leg. What are the lengths of all three sides of the fountain?

   _____

LESSON 4-3
Problem Solving with Constraints
Practice and Problem Solving: C

In Problems 1–6, solve for the missing information.

1. The diameter of a cylindrical water tank is half the measure of the cylinder's height. The tank has a volume of 1570 cubic feet. Find the height of the tank. Use 3.14 for π.

   _____

2. The height of a bookcase is $2\frac{1}{2}$ times the width. The depth is $\frac{1}{3}$ of the width. The volume of the cabinet is 22,500 in^3. What are the bookshelf's dimensions?

   _____

3. Concrete costs $105 per cubic yard. Alice is making a rectangular patio measuring 20 feet long by 16 feet wide. The cost of the concrete for her patio floor is $622.22. How thick is the patio floor (rounded to the nearest inch)?

   _____

4. A swimming pool in the shape of a rectangular prism has a bottom, no top, two square sides, and two rectangular sides with a length equal to twice the length of the square sides. All four sides share a common height. The total area of the five sides is 288 ft^2. Find the volume of the swimming pool.

   _____

5. Sean's filing cabinet is 1 foot wide and 3 feet high. The folders that he keeps in the file cabinet are 12 inches wide, 1 inch thick, and 9 inches tall. The file cabinet can hold 144 of these folders. How deep is the file cabinet?

   _____

6. A 5-foot-tall cylindrical container with a diameter of 6 inches is filled with a gas that costs $60 per cubic foot. What is the total value of the gas in the container if it is filled completely?

   _____

Name _____ Date _____ Class_____

LESSON 5-1 **Transformations of Function Graphs**

Practice and Problem Solving: A/B

Let $g(x)$ be the transformation of $f(x)$. Write the rule for $g(x)$ using the change described.

1. reflection across the y-axis followed by a vertical shift 3 units up _____

2. horizontal stretch by a factor of 5 followed by a horizontal shift right 2 units _____

3. vertical compression by a factor of $\frac{1}{8}$ followed by a vertical shift down 6 units _____

4. reflection across the x-axis followed by a vertical stretch by a factor of 2, a horizontal shift 7 units left, and a vertical shift 5 units down _____

Use the graph to perform each transformation.

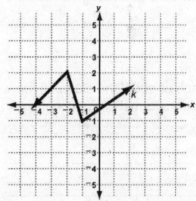

5. Transform $y = k(x)$ by compressing it horizontally by a factor of $\frac{1}{2}$. Label the new function $m(x)$. Which coordinate is multiplied by $\frac{1}{2}$?

_____

6. Transform $y = k(x)$ by translating it down 3 units. Label the new function $p(x)$. What happens to the y-coordinate in each new ordered pair?

_____

7. Transform $y = k(x)$ by stretching it vertically by a factor of 2. Label the new function $q(x)$. Which coordinate is multiplied by 2?

_____

8. Describe how the coordinates of a function change when the function is translated 2 units to the left and 4 units up. _____

LESSON 5-1 Transformations of Function Graphs

Practice and Problem Solving: C

Recall the graph of the ceiling function $f(x) = \lceil x \rceil$, shown.
The following situation describes a transformation of $f(x)$:

To rent a concert hall for one hour costs $40 plus an initial cleaning fee of $120. There is a charge of $40 for every additional hour or fraction of an hour thereafter.

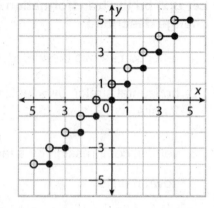

Use the description for Problems 1–6.

1. Write a transformation function $g(x)$ in terms of $f(x)$

   describing the cost of renting the concert hall.

   _____

2. Graph $g(x)$. Show the rental cost for up to 8 hours.

3. Describe the effect on the graph of $g(x)$ if the cleaning fee were changed to $80. Then write a transformation function $h(x)$ in terms of $g(x)$ based on this situation.

   _____

   _____

4. Graph $h(x)$. Show the rental cost for up to 8 hours.

5. Describe the effect on the graph of $g(x)$ if the rental fees were changed to $40 for every 2 hours. Then write a transformation function $j(x)$ in terms of $g(x)$ based on this situation.

   _____

   _____

6. Graph $j(x)$. Show the rental cost for up to 8 hours.

Name _____ Date _____ Class_____

LESSON
5-2
Inverses of Functions
Practice and Problem Solving: A/B

Find the inverse of each function.

1. $f(x) = 10 - 4x$ _____

2. $g(x) = 15x - 10$ _____

3. $h(x) = \dfrac{x - 12}{4}$ _____

4. $j(x) = \dfrac{3x + 1}{6}$ _____

Find the inverse of each function. Then graph the function and its inverse.

5. $f(x) = 5x + 10$ 6. $f(x) = \dfrac{9}{2}x - 5$

$f^{-1}(x) =$ _____ $f^{-1}(x) =$ _____

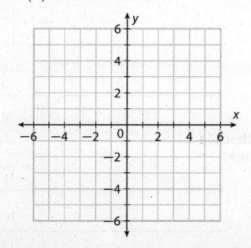 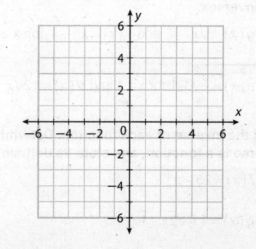

Use composition to determine whether each pair of functions are inverses.

7. $g(x) = -5 - \dfrac{7}{2}x$ and $f(x) = -\dfrac{2}{7}x - \dfrac{10}{7}$ _____

8. $s(x) = 7 - 2x$ and $t(x) = \dfrac{1}{2}x + \dfrac{7}{2}$ _____

9. $h(x) = \dfrac{1}{3}x + 4$ and $j(x) = 3x - 12$ _____

Name _____ Date _____ Class_____

Inverses of Functions

Practice and Problem Solving: C

**Determine whether the inverse of each relation is a function.
If so, state whether the inverse is a one-to-one or a many-to-one
function. If not, explain the reasoning.**

1.

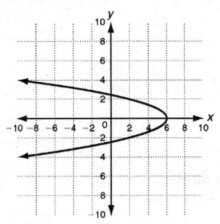

_____

2.

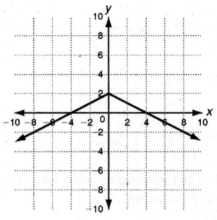

_____

**Use composition to determine whether each pair of functions
are inverses.**

3. $g(x) = \sqrt{x} - 4$ and $r(x) = x^2 + 4$ for $x \geq 0$ _____

4. $u(x) = \dfrac{x^2}{4} - 1$ for $x \geq 1$ and $v(x) = \pm 2\sqrt{x+1}$ _____

**Find the inverse of each function. Determine whether the
inverse is a function, and state its domain and range.**

5. $f(x) = 25 - x^2$ _____

6. $g(x) = 4 + \sqrt{2x - 1}$ _____

**The area of a regular octagon can be found using the
formula $A(s) = 2s^2\left(\sqrt{2} + 1\right)$, where s is the length of each side.
Use this information for Problems 7–9.**

7. Find the inverse, $A^{-1}(s)$. _____

8. What does the inverse represent? _____

9. What is the side length of a regular octagon
   whose area is $\left(9.68\sqrt{2} + 9.68\right)$ square meters? _____

**LESSON
5-3**

Graphing Cubic Functions
Practice and Problem Solving: A/B

Calculate the reference points for each transformation of the parent function $f(x) = x^3$. Then graph the transformation. (The graph of the parent function is shown.)

1. $g(x) = (x-3)^3 + 2$

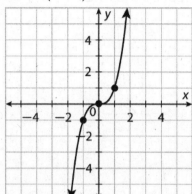

_____

2. $g(x) = -3(x+2)^3 - 2$

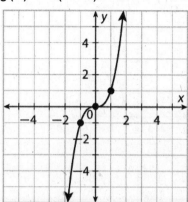

_____

Write the equation of the cubic function whose graph is shown.

3.

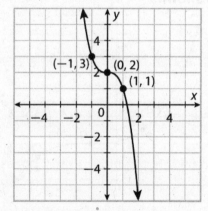

_____

4.

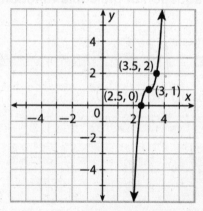

_____

Solve.

5. The graph of $f(x) = x^3$ is reflected across the *x*-axis. The graph is then translated 11 units up and 7 units to the left. Write the equation of the transformed function.

_____

6. The graph of $f(x) = x^3$ is stretched vertically by a factor of 6. The graph is then translated 9 units to the right and 3 units down. Write the equation of the transformed function.

_____

LESSON 5-3

Graphing Cubic Functions

Practice and Problem Solving: C

Calculate the reference points for each transformation of the parent function $f(x) = x^3$. Then graph the transformation. (The graph of the parent function is shown.)

1. $g(x) = -\dfrac{5}{2}(x-3)^3 + \dfrac{1}{2}$

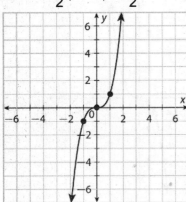

_____

2. $g(x) = 1.25(x+5)^3 - 1.25$

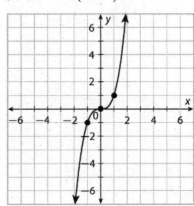

_____

Write the equation of the cubic function whose graph is shown.

3.

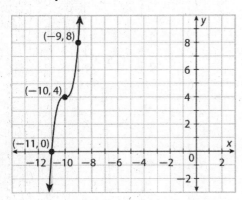

_____

4.

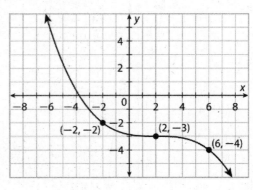

_____

Solve.

5. The graph of the function $y = 3(x-2)^3 + 7$ is translated 2 units to the right and then 4 units down. Write the equation of the final graph.

_____

6. The graph of the function $y = (x)^3 + 5$ is translated 2 units to the left and then reflected across the x-axis. Write the equation of the final graph.

_____

LESSON 5-4

Graphing Polynomial Functions

Practice and Problem Solving: A/B

Identify whether the function graphed has an odd or even degree and a positive or negative leading coefficient.

1.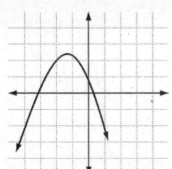

_____

2.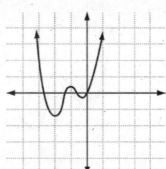

_____

3.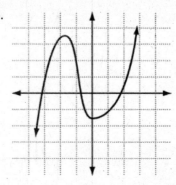

_____

Use a graphing calculator to determine the number of turning points and the number and type (global or local) of any maximum or minimum values.

4. $f(x) = x(x-4)^2$

_____

5. $f(x) = -x^2(x-2)(x+1)$

_____

Graph the function. State the end behavior, *x*-intercepts, and intervals where the function is above or below the *x*-axis.

6. $f(x) = -(x-1)^2(x+3)$

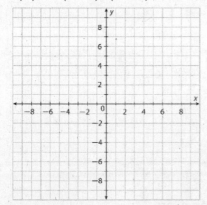

End behavior: _____

x-intercepts: _____

Above *x*-axis: _____

Below *x* axis: _____

7. $f(x) = (x+2)(x-3)(x-1)$

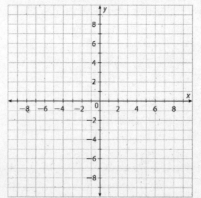

End behavior: _____

x-intercepts: _____

Above *x*-axis: _____

Below *x*-axis: _____

LESSON
5-4

Graphing Polynomial Functions

Practice and Problem Solving: C

Identify whether the function graphed has an odd or even degree and a positive or negative leading coefficient.

1.
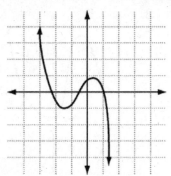
_____

2.
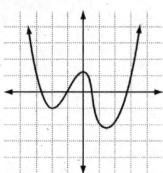
_____

3.
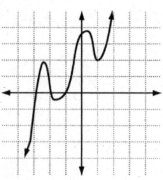
_____

Use a graphing calculator to determine the number of turning points and the number and type (global or local) of any maximum or minimum values.

4. $f(x) = -(x-1)^3(x+2)$

_____

5. $f(x) = x^5(x-3)(x+2)$

_____

Graph the function. State the end behavior, *x*-intercepts, and intervals where the function is above or below the *x*-axis.

6. $f(x) = (x-2)^2(x+2)(x+3)$

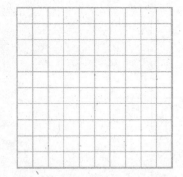

7. $f(x) = -(x-1)^3(x+2)^2(x-3)$

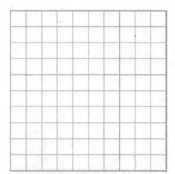

End behavior: _____

x-intercepts: _____

Above x-axis: _____

Below x axis: _____

End behavior: _____

x-intercepts: _____

Above x-axis: _____

Below x-axis: _____

LESSON	Adding and Subtracting Polynomials
6-1	*Practice and Problem Solving: A/B*

Identify the degree of each monomial.

1. $6x^2$

2. $3p^3m^4$

3. $2x^8y^3$

_____   _____   _____

Rewrite each polynomial in standard form. Then identify the leading coefficient, degree, and number of terms.

4. $6 + 7x - 4x^3 + x^2$

_____

5. $x^2 - 3 + 2x^5 + 7x^4 - 12x$

_____

Add or subtract. Write your answer in standard form.

6. $(2x^2 - 2x + 6) + (11x^3 - x^2 - 2 + 5x)$ 7. $(x^2 - 8) - (3x^3 - 6x - 4 + 9x^2)$

_____   _____

8. $(5x^4 + x^2) + (7 + 9x^2 - 2x^4 + x^3)$ 9. $(12x^2 + x) - (6 - 9x^2 + x^7 - 8x)$

_____   _____

Solve.

10. An accountant finds that the gross income, in thousands of dollars, of a small business can be modeled by the polynomial $-0.3t^2 + 8t + 198$, where t is the number of years after 2010. The yearly expenses of the business, in thousands of dollars, can be modeled by the polynomial $-0.2t^2 + 2t + 131$.

    a. Find a polynomial that predicts the net profit of the business after t years.

      _____

    b. Assuming that the models continue to hold, how much net profit can the business expect to make in the year 2016?

      _____

Adding and Subtracting Polynomials

Practice and Problem Solving: C

Rewrite each polynomial in standard form. Then identify the leading coefficient, degree, and number of terms.

1. $5x^3 + 2x - 1 - 10x^2 + 9x^5 - 3x^4$

_____

Add or subtract. Write your answer in standard form.

2. $(7x^3 + 2x - 1) + (8x^2 - 6 + 2x - x^3)$

_____

3. $(12 - 11x - 5x^5) - (4x^4 + 8x - 4x^5 + 2x^3 - 1)$

_____

4. $(-3x^4 + x^6 - 9x^5 + 2x^2 - 7) - (-2x^5 + x - 4x^2 - x^4 + 12)$

_____

Solve.

5. What polynomial could you add to $3x^4 - 9x^3 + 5x^2 - x + 7$ to get a sum of $3 + 4x^4 + 3x - x^3 + 3x^2$?

_____

6. What polynomial could you subtract from $5x^3 - 12x - x^2 + 9 - 12x^5 - 6x^4$ to give a difference of $19 + 8x^3 - 18x - 19x^5 - 2x^2 - 8x^4$?

_____

7. The profit earned by the sales division of a company each year can be modeled by the polynomial $x^3 - x^2 + 2x - 100$, where x is the number of units sold. The profit earned by the manufacturing division can be modeled with the polynomial $x^2 - 4x - 300$.

   a. Write a polynomial to represent the difference of the profit from the sales division and the profit from the manufacturing division.

   _____

   b. What is the total amount of profit that the company earns from both divisions?

   _____

LESSON 6-2 Multiplying Polynomials
Practice and Problem Solving: A/B

Find each product.

1. $4x^2(3x^2 + 1)$

   _____

2. $-9x(x^2 + 2x + 4)$

   _____

3. $-6x^2(x^3 + 7x^2 - 4x + 3)$

   _____

4. $x^3(-4x^3 + 10x^2 - 7x + 2)$

   _____

5. $-5m^3(7n^4 - 2mn^3 + 6)$

   _____

6. $(x + 2)(y^2 + 2y - 12)$

   _____

7. $(p + q)(4p^2 - p - 8q^2 - q)$

   _____

8. $(2x^2 + xy - y)(y^2 + 3x)$

   _____

Expand each expression.

9. $(3x - 1)^3$

   _____

10. $(x - 4)^4$

    _____

11. $3(a - 4b)^2$

    _____

12. $5(x^2 - 2y)^3$

    _____

Solve.

13. A biologist has found that the number of branches on a certain rare tree
    in its first few years of life can be modeled by the polynomial
    $b(y) = 4y^2 + y$. The number of leaves on each branch can be modeled
    by the polynomial $l(y) = 2y^3 + 3y^2 + y$, where y is the number of years
    after the tree reaches a height of 6 feet. Write a polynomial describing
    the total number of leaves on the tree.

    _____

LESSON 6-2

Multiplying Polynomials
Practice and Problem Solving: C

Consider the expansion of $(x + y)^n$.

1. How many terms does the expression contain? _____

2. What is the exponent of x in the first term? _____

3. What is the exponent of y in the first term? _____

4. What is the sum of the exponents in any term of the expansion? _____

Find each product.

5. $-y^3(10x^2 + 4xy - y^2)$

6. $(2a - b)^3$

7. $5(h - 2)^4$

8. $(2m^2 + n)(3n^2 + 6mn - m^2)$

9. $\left(\frac{1}{3}x + 4\right)^3$

10. $(4x - 5)(2x^5 + x^3 - 1)$

11. $(a^3 + a^2b^2)(b^4 + a^2)$

12. $(k^4 + k^3 + 12)(k^2 - k - 9)$

Solve.

13. The momentum of an object is defined as its mass m multiplied by its velocity. As a certain experimental aircraft burns fuel, its mass decreases according to the polynomial $m(t) = 3000 - 0.1t^2 - 4t$, where m is in kilograms and t is measured in minutes since takeoff. Under the force of the engines, the velocity of the aircraft increases according to the function $v(t) = 0.001t^3 + 0.01t$, where v is in kilometers per second. What is the momentum of the rocket?

_____

LESSON
6-3

The Binomial Theorem

Practice and Problem Solving: A/B

Use the Binomial Theorem to expand each binomial.

1. $(x + y)^3$

_____

2. $(2x + y)^4$

_____

3. $(m + 3n)^3$

_____

4. $(p + q)^5$

_____

Solve.

5. Of the new cars in a car dealer's lot, 1 in 6 are white. Today, 4 cars were sold.

   a. What is the probability that 3 of the cars sold were white?

   _____

   b. What is the probability that at least 2 of the cars sold were white?

   _____

6. At a small college, $\dfrac{1}{3}$ of all of the students are vegetarians. There are
5 students in line at the cafeteria.

   a. What is the probability that all 5 students are vegetarians?

   _____

   b. What is the probability that just 1 of the students is a vegetarian?

   _____

7. Ellen plays 8 hands of a card game with her friends. She has a 1 in 3
chance of winning each hand. What is the probability that she will win
exactly half of the hands played?

_____

8. In a lottery, each ticket buyer has a 1 in 10 chance of winning a prize.
If Chip buys 10 tickets, what is the probability that he will win at least
1 prize?

_____

Name _____ Date _____ Class_____

The Binomial Theorem

Practice and Problem Solving: C

Use the Binomial Theorem to expand each binomial.

1. $(x + y)^5$

_____

2. $(4x + y)^4$

_____

3. $(2x + y)^5$

_____

4. $(n + 2m)^4$

_____

Solve.

5. At Hopewell High School, 1 in 7 students is on a sports team. There are 4 student council representatives in the school.

   a. What is the probability that 2 of the student council representatives are also on a sports team?

   _____

   b. What is the probability that at least 3 of the student council representatives are on a sports team?

   _____

6. A donut shop sells donuts with a jelly filling. Two in every 5 donuts have a jelly filling. There are 5 donuts left in the package.

   a. What is the probability that all 5 donuts have a jelly filling?

   _____

   b. What is the probability that none of the donuts has a jelly filling?

   _____

7. Andrew is choosing CDs from a bag of free CDs without looking. He has a 1 in 5 chance of choosing a CD that he likes. He chooses 8 CDs in all. What is the probability that he will get 3 CDs that he likes?

   _____

8. In a game of bingo, the contestants have a 1 in 12 chance of winning each round. If Shirley plays 6 rounds, what is the probability that she will win at least half of them?

   _____

LESSON 6-4 Factoring Polynomials

Practice and Problem Solving: A/B

Simplify each polynomial, if possible. Then factor it.

1. $3n^2 - 48$

2. $3x^3 - 75x$

3. $9m^4 - 16$

4. $16r^4 - 9$

5. $3n^6 - 12$

6. $x^6 - 9$

7. $3b^7 + 12b^4 + 12b$

8. $50v^6 + 60v^3 + 18$

9. $x^3 - 64$

10. $x^3 - 125$

11. $x^6 - 64$

12. $x^6 - 1$

Factor each polynomial by grouping.

13. $8n^3 - 7n^2 + 56n - 49$

14. $5x^3 - 6x^2 - 15x + 18$

15. $9r^3 + 3r^2 - 21r - 7$

16. $25v^3 + 25v^2 - 15v - 15$

17. $120b^3 + 105b^2 + 200b + 175$

18. $120x^3 - 80x^2 - 168x + 112$

Solve.

19. A square concert stage in the center of a fairground has an area
of $4x^2 + 12x + 9$ ft². The dimensions of the stage have the form
$cx + d$, where c and d are whole numbers. Find an expression for
the perimeter of the stage. What is the perimeter when $x = 2$ ft?

Factoring Polynomials

LESSON 6-4

Practice and Problem Solving: C

Simplify each polynomial. Then factor it.

1. $12v^4 - 75$

2. $5p^6 - 80$

3. $20u^6 - 20u^3v^3 + 5v^6$

4. $4x^6 - 32x^3y^3 + 64y^6$

5. $8x^3 + 125$

6. $64x^6 - 1$

Factor each polynomial by grouping. Be sure to factor the polynomial completely.

7. $b^3 - 2b^2 - b + 2$

8. $24v^3 + 56v^2 - 15v - 35$

9. $245n^3 - 175n^2 - 196n + 140$

10. $140x^6 + 100x^5 - 28x^4 - 20x^3$

11. $150u^2v + 75u - 125u^2 - 90uv$

12. $196x^2y - 64x + 56x^2 - 224xy$

Solve.

13. Fatima has an herb garden. She grows parsley in a triangular section having an area of $\frac{1}{2}(3x^2 - 6x - x + 2)$ ft^2. What are the dimensions for the base and height of the parsley section?

14. The voltage generated by an electrical circuit changes over time according to the polynomial $V(t) = t^3 - 4t^2 - 25t + 100$, where V is in volts and t is in seconds. Factor the polynomial to find the times when the voltage is equal to zero.

Dividing Polynomials
Practice and Problem Solving: A/B

Divide by using long division.

1. $(x^2 - x - 6) \div (x - 3)$

2. $(2x^3 - 10x^2 + x - 5) \div (x - 5)$

_____

3. $(-3x^2 + 20x - 12) \div (x - 6)$

4. $(3x^3 + 9x^2 - 14) \div (x + 3)$

_____

Divide by using synthetic division.

5. $(3x^2 - 8x + 4) \div (x - 2)$

6. $(5x^2 - 4x + 12) \div (x + 3)$

_____

7. $(9x^2 - 7x + 3) \div (x - 1)$

8. $(-6x^2 + 5x - 10) \div (x + 7)$

_____

Use synthetic substitution to evaluate $P(x)$ for the given value.

9. $P(x) = 4x^2 - 9x + 2$ for $x = 3$

10. $P(x) = -3x^2 + 10x - 4$ for $x = -2$

_____

Determine whether the given binomial is a factor of $P(x)$.

11. $(x - 4)$; $P(x) = x^2 + 8x - 48$

12. $(x + 5)$; $P(x) = 2x^2 - 6x - 1$

_____

Solve.

13. The total number of dollars donated each year to a small charitable organization
has followed the trend $d(t) = 2t^3 + 10t^2 + 2000t + 10,000$, where d is dollars and t
is the number of years since 1990. The total number of donors each year has
followed the trend $p(t) = t^2 + 1000$. Write an expression describing the average
number of dollars per donor.

_____

LESSON 6-5

Dividing Polynomials

Practice and Problem Solving: C

Divide by using long division.

1. $(2x^3 + 14x^2 - 4x - 48) \div (2x + 4)$

2. $(x^3 + 12x^2 - 4) \div (x - 3)$

_____

_____

3. $(12x^4 + 23x^3 - 9x^2 + 15x + 4) \div (3x - 1)$

4. $(-2x^3 + 11x^2 - 8x - 7) \div (2x + 1)$

_____

_____

Divide by using synthetic division.

5. $(9x^2 - 3x + 11) \div (x - 6)$

6. $(3x^4 - 2x^2 + 1) \div (x + 2)$

_____

_____

7. $(6x^5 - 3x^2 + x - 2) \div (x - 1)$

8. $(-x^4 - 7x^3 + 6x^2 - 1) \div (x - 3)$

_____

_____

Use synthetic substitution to evaluate $P(x)$ for the given value.

9. $P(x) = 4x^3 - 12x - 2$ for $x = 5$

10. $P(x) = -3x^4 + 5x^3 - x + 7$ for $x = -2$

_____

_____

Use the Factor Theorem to verify that the given binomial is a factor of $P(x)$. Then divide.

11. $(x + 5); P(x) = 2x^2 + 6x - 20$

12. $(x - 1); P(x) = x^4 - 6x^3 + 4x^2 + 1$

_____

_____

Solve.

13. The total weight of the cargo entering a seaport each year can be modeled by the function $C(t) = 0.2t^3 + 1000t^2 + 10t + 50,000$, where t is the number of years since the port was opened. The average weight of cargo delivered by each ship is modeled by the function $A(t) = 0.1t + 500$. Write an expression describing the number of ships entering the port each year.

_____

LESSON 7-1
Finding Rational Solutions of Polynomial Equations
Practice and Problem Solving: A/B

Solve each polynomial equation by factoring.

1. $4x^3 + x^2 - 4x - 1 = 0$

_____

2. $x^5 - 2x^4 - 24x^3 = 0$

_____

3. $3x^5 + 18x^4 - 21x^3 = 0$

_____

4. $-x^4 + 2x^3 + 8x^2 = 0$

_____

Identify the rational zeros of each function. Then write the function in factored form.

5. $f(x) = x^3 + 3x^2 + 3x + 1$

_____

6. $f(x) = x^3 + 5x^2 - 8x - 48$

_____

Identify all the rational roots of each equation.

7. $x^3 + 10x^2 + 17x = 28$

_____

8. $3x^3 + 10x^2 - 27x = 10$

_____

Solve.

9. An engineer is designing a storage compartment in a spacecraft. The compartment must be 2 meters longer than it is wide, and its depth must be 1 meter less than its width. The volume of the compartment must be 8 cubic meters.

   a. Write an equation to model the volume of the compartment.

   _____

   b. List all possible rational roots. _____

   c. Use synthetic division to find the roots of the polynomial equation. Are the roots all rational numbers?

   _____

   d. What are the dimensions of the storage compartment? _____

LESSON 7-1 Finding Rational Solutions of Polynomial Equations
Practice and Problem Solving: C

Solve each polynomial equation by factoring.

1. $-3x^4 + 6x^3 + 105x^2 = 0$

2. $8x^7 - 56x^6 + 96x^5 = 0$

_____   _____

Identify the rational zeros of each function. Then write the function in factored form.

3. $f(x) = x^3 + 6x^2 + 12x - 8$

4. $f(x) = x^3 + 10x^2 + 32x + 32$

_____   _____

Identify all the rational roots of each equation.

5. $x^3 + 2x^2 - 48x = 0$

6. $5x^4 + 19x^3 - 29x^2 + 5x = 0$

_____   _____

7. $6x^3 + 12x^2 - 18x = 0$

8. $3x^4 + 5x^3 - 11x^2 + 3x = 0$

_____   _____

Solve.

9. A jewelry box is designed such that its length is twice its width and its depth is 2 inches less than its width. The volume of the box is 64 cubic inches.

   a. Write an equation to model the volume of the box.

   _____

   b. List all possible rational roots. _____

   c. Use synthetic division to find the roots of the polynomial equation. Are the roots all rational numbers?

   _____

   d. What are the dimensions of the box? _____

LESSON 7-2

Finding Complex Solutions of Polynomial Equations

Practice and Problem Solving: A/B

Write the simplest polynomial function with the given roots.

1. 1, 4, and −3

2. $\frac{1}{2}$, 5, and −2

3. $2i$, $\sqrt{3}$, and 4

4. $\sqrt{2}$, −5, and −3i

Solve each equation by finding all roots.

5. $x^4 - 2x^3 - 14x^2 - 2x - 15 = 0$

6. $x^4 - 16 = 0$

7. $x^4 + 4x^3 + 4x^2 + 64x - 192 = 0$

8. $x^3 + 3x^2 + 9x + 27 = 0$

Solve.

9. An electrical circuit is designed such that its output voltage, V, measured in volts, can be either positive or negative. The voltage of the circuit passes through zero at $t = 1$, 2, and 7 seconds. Write the simplest polynomial describing the voltage $V(t)$.

Finding Complex Solutions of Polynomial Equations
Practice and Problem Solving: C

Write the simplest polynomial function with the given roots.

1. $-\dfrac{3}{4}, 6,$ and -1

2. $-5i, 2,$ and 7

_____   _____

3. $-i, -3,$ and -1

4. $2i, 4,$ and $\sqrt{6}$

_____   _____

Solve each equation by finding all roots.

5. $4x^4 - 8x^3 - 3x^2 - 18x - 27 = 0$

6. $x^4 + 3x^3 - x^2 + 9x - 12 = 0$

_____   _____

7. $x^4 - 3x^3 - 8x^2 + 22x - 24 = 0$

8. $x^3 + 6x^2 + 4x + 24 = 0$

_____   _____

Solve.

9. For a scientific experiment, Tony needs a glass bell jar in the shape of
   a cylinder with a hemisphere on top. The height of the cylinder must be
   3 inches longer than its radius, and the volume must be 72π cubic
   inches. What should the radius of the cylinder be?

_____

LESSON 8-1 Graphing Simple Rational Functions

Practice and Problem Solving: A/B

Using the graph of $f(x) = \dfrac{1}{x}$ as a guide, describe the transformation and graph the function.

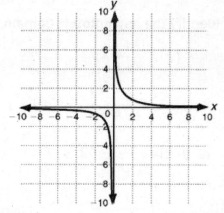

1. $g(x) = \dfrac{2}{x+4}$

_____

Identify the asymptotes, domain, and range of each function.

2. $g(x) = \dfrac{1}{x-3} + 5$ _____

_____

3. $g(x) = \dfrac{1}{x+8} - 1$ _____

_____

Identify the asymptotes of the function. Then graph.

4. $f(x) = \dfrac{x^2 + 4x - 5}{x+1}$

   a. Vertical asymptote:

   _____

   b. Horizontal asymptote:

   _____

   c. Graph.

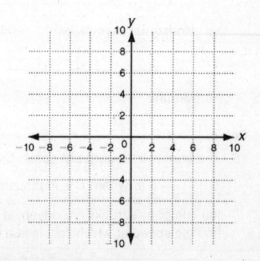

Solve.

5. The number *n* of daily visitors to a new store can be modeled by the function
$n = \dfrac{(250x + 1000)}{x}$, where *x* is the number of days the store has been open.

   a. What is the horizontal asymptote of this function
and what does it represent? _____

   b. To the nearest integer, how many
visitors can be expected on day 30? _____

LESSON
8-1

Graphing Simple Rational Functions

Practice and Problem Solving: C

Identify the asymptotes, domain, and range of each function.

1. $g(x) = \dfrac{1}{x+5} + 7$ _____

2. $g(x) = \dfrac{4}{x-9} - \dfrac{1}{4}$ _____

3. $g(x) = \dfrac{1}{x + \dfrac{2}{3}} - 12$ _____

Identify the zeros and asymptotes of the function. Then graph.

4. $f(x) = \dfrac{x^2 - 4x + 3}{4x + 4}$

   a. Zeros:

   b. Vertical asymptote:

     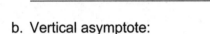

   c. Horizontal asymptote:

     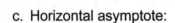

   d. Graph.

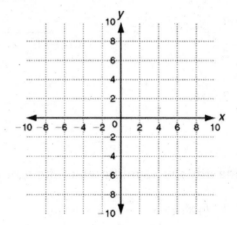

Solve.

5. The annual transportation costs, *C*, incurred by a company follow the formula

   $C = \dfrac{2500}{s} + s$, where *C* is in thousands of dollars and *s* is the average speed

   the company's trucks are driven, in miles per hour. Use your graphing calculator to
   find the speed at which cost is at a minimum.

_____

LESSON
8-2

Graphing More Complicated Rational Functions

Practice and Problem Solving: A/B

Identify all vertical asymptotes and holes of each rational function. Then state its domain.

1. $f(x) = \dfrac{x-1}{-3x^2+27}$

   Vertical Asymptotes: _____

   Holes: _____

   Domain: _____

2. $f(x) = \dfrac{-x^2-3x+4}{x^2+2x-8}$

   Vertical Asymptotes: _____

   Holes: _____

   Domain: _____

Determine the end behavior of each rational function.

3. $f(x) = \dfrac{x^2-4}{-3x}$

4. $f(x) = \dfrac{x^2+5x+6}{x^2+7x+12}$

_____

_____

Identify the asymptotes, holes, and *x*-intercepts of each rational function. Then graph the function.

5. $f(x) = \dfrac{x+2}{-2x^2-6x}$

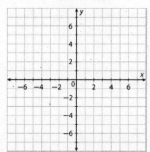

6. $f(x) = \dfrac{-x^2+1}{x^2-3x+2}$

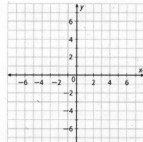

Vertical Asymptotes: _____

Horizontal Asymptotes: _____

Holes: _____

x-intercept(s): _____

Vertical Asymptotes: _____

Horizontal Asymptotes: _____

Holes: _____

x-intercept(s): _____

LESSON
8-2

Graphing More Complicated Rational Functions

Practice and Problem Solving: C

Identify all vertical asymptotes and holes of each rational function. Then state its domain.

1. $f(x) = \dfrac{x^2 + 5x + 4}{-4x^2 + 4x + 24}$

   Vertical Asymptotes: _____

   Holes: _____

   Domain: _____

2. $f(x) = \dfrac{x^3 + 2x^2 - 3x}{-3x^2 - 12x - 9}$

   Vertical Asymptotes: _____

   Holes: _____

   Domain: _____

Determine the end behavior of each rational function.

3. $f(x) = \dfrac{x^2 - x - 2}{-3x}$

   _____

4. $f(x) = \dfrac{-3x^2 + 3x + 6}{x^2 - 2x - 3}$

   _____

Identify the asymptotes, holes, and *x*-intercepts of each rational function. Then graph the function.

5. $f(x) = \dfrac{-4x^2 + 4x}{x^3 - 5x^2 + 4x}$

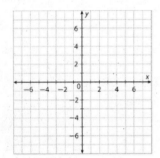

   Vertical Asymptotes: _____

   Horizontal Asymptotes: _____

   Holes: _____

   x-intercept(s): _____

6. $f(x) = \dfrac{x^3 - 9x}{x^3 - 7x^2 + 12x}$

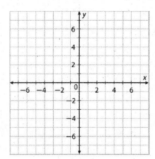

   Vertical Asymptotes: _____

   Horizontal Asymptotes: _____

   Holes: _____

   x-intercept(s): _____

LESSON
9-1

Adding and Subtracting Rational Expressions
Practice and Problem Solving: A/B

Identify the excluded values for each expression.

1. $\dfrac{x-7}{9x^2-63x}$

2. $\dfrac{x^2+3x-18}{-x^2+6x-9}$

_____   _____

Simplify the given expression stating any excluded values.

3. $\dfrac{2x^2-12x+16}{7x^2-28x}$

4. $\dfrac{5x^2+6x-8}{6x^2-24}$

_____   _____

5. $\dfrac{9x^3+9x^2}{7x^2-2x-9}$

6. $\dfrac{2x^2+13x-24}{7x+56}$

_____   _____

Add or subtract. Identify any *x*-values for which the expression is undefined.

7. $\dfrac{2x-3}{x+4}+\dfrac{4x-5}{x+4}$

8. $\dfrac{x+12}{2x-5}-\dfrac{3x-2}{2x-5}$

_____   _____

9. $\dfrac{x+4}{x^2-x-12}+\dfrac{2x}{x-4}$

10. $\dfrac{3x^2-1}{x^2-3x-18}-\dfrac{x+2}{x-6}$

_____   _____

11. $\dfrac{x+2}{x^2-2x-15}+\dfrac{x}{x+3}$

12. $\dfrac{x+6}{x^2-7x-18}-\dfrac{2x}{x-9}$

_____   _____

Solve.

13. A messenger is required to deliver 10 packages per day. Each day, the
messenger works only for as long as it takes to deliver the daily quota
of 10 packages. On average, the messenger is able to deliver 2
packages per hour on Saturday and 4 packages per hour on Sunday.
What is the messenger's average delivery rate on the weekend?

_____

LESSON 9-1

Adding and Subtracting Rational Expressions

Practice and Problem Solving: C

Identify the excluded values for each expression.

1. $\dfrac{7x^2 - 47x + 30}{3x^2 - 24x + 36}$

   _____

2. $\dfrac{2x^3 - 8x^2 - 64x}{5x^2 - 50x + 80}$

   _____

Simplify the given expression stating any excluded values .

3. $\dfrac{7x - 21}{15x^2 - 18x - 81}$

   _____

4. $\dfrac{6x^3 - 24x}{10x^3 + 2x^2 - 12x}$

   _____

5. $\dfrac{7x^2 - 14x + 7}{2x^2 - 4x + 2}$

   _____

6. $\dfrac{10x^3 + 60x^2}{15x^2 + 105x + 90}$

   _____

Add or subtract. Identify any *x*-values for which the expression is undefined.

7. $\dfrac{5x - 1}{x + 3} + \dfrac{3x}{2x + 6}$

   _____

8. $\dfrac{7x}{3x^2} - \dfrac{2}{x + 4}$

   _____

9. $\dfrac{x}{x - 4} + \dfrac{x + 1}{3x + 1}$

   _____

10. $\dfrac{3}{x - 5} - \dfrac{1}{x^2 - 7x + 10}$

    _____

11. $\dfrac{x}{4x - 2} + \dfrac{3x + 3}{4x + 2}$

    _____

12. $\dfrac{3x}{x^2 - x - 6} - \dfrac{5}{x^2 - 8x + 15}$

    _____

Solve.

13. The electric potential generated by a certain arrangement of electric charges is given by $\dfrac{e}{x - 4} + \dfrac{e}{x + 1}$, where *e* is the fundamental unit of electric charge and *x* measures the location where the potential is being measured. Express the electric potential as a rational expression.

_____

Multiplying and Dividing Rational Expressions
Practice and Problem Solving: A/B

Multiply. State any excluded values.

1. $\dfrac{6x}{10} \cdot \dfrac{6x}{3x^3}$

_____

2. $\dfrac{4x}{3} \cdot \dfrac{8x}{2}$

_____

3. $\dfrac{1}{x+9} \cdot \dfrac{7x^3 + 49x^2}{x+7}$

_____

4. $\dfrac{6x^2 - 54x}{x-9} \cdot \dfrac{7x}{6x}$

_____

5. $\dfrac{18x - 36}{4x - 8} \cdot \dfrac{2}{9x + 18}$

_____

6. $\left(56 + 11x - 15x^2\right) \cdot \dfrac{10}{15x^2 - 11x - 56}$

_____

Divide. State any excluded values.

7. $\dfrac{4x}{5x} \div \dfrac{4x}{6}$

_____

8. $\dfrac{6(x-2)}{(x-1)(x-10)} \div \dfrac{x-2}{x-10}$

_____

9. $(2x + 6) \div \dfrac{14x^2 + 42x}{10}$

_____

10. $\dfrac{27x + 9}{10} \div \dfrac{3x^2 - 8x - 3}{10}$

_____

11. $\dfrac{24x + 56}{10x^3 - 90x^2} \div \dfrac{15x + 35}{5}$

_____

12. $\dfrac{2x + 20}{12x^3 - 30x^2} \div \dfrac{2}{14x - 35}$

_____

Solve.

13. The distance, *d*, traveled by a car undergoing constant acceleration, *a*, for a time, *t*, is given by $d = v_0 t + \dfrac{1}{2}at^2$, where v_0 is the initial velocity of the car. Two cars are side by side with the same initial velocity. One car accelerates, $a = A$, and the other car does not accelerate, $a = 0$. Write an expression for the ratio of the distance traveled by the accelerating car to the distance traveled by the nonaccelerating car as a function of time.

_____

Multiplying and Dividing Rational Expressions
Practice and Problem Solving: C

Multiply. State any excluded values.

1. $\dfrac{27x}{19x} \cdot \dfrac{12x^4}{11}$

2. $\dfrac{14x^2}{15x} \cdot \dfrac{41x}{49}$

_____

_____

3. $\dfrac{169x^2 + 104x - 48}{44x^3} \cdot \dfrac{x - 11}{169x^2 + 104x - 48}$

4. $\dfrac{3x + 5}{15x^2 + 34x + 15} \cdot \dfrac{5x^2 - 62x - 39}{5x^2 - 50x}$

_____

_____

5. $\dfrac{5x - 8}{2x^2 + 14x + 20} \cdot \dfrac{20x^2 + 40x}{15x^2 - 24x}$

6. $\dfrac{15x^2 + 12x}{40x + 32} \cdot \dfrac{7x - 14}{3x}$

_____

_____

Divide. State any excluded values.

7. $\dfrac{14x^2}{6x^3} \div \dfrac{7}{3x}$

8. $\dfrac{5(x + 13)}{x + 13} \div \dfrac{5x - 30}{14x^2}$

_____

_____

9. $\dfrac{84x^2}{7x + 10} \div \dfrac{11x + 132}{77x + 110}$

10. $\dfrac{2x^2 + 10x - 12}{22x^2 - 42x + 20} \div \dfrac{1}{11x^2 + 100x - 100}$

_____

_____

11. $\dfrac{77x + 11}{3x - 42} \div \dfrac{21x + 3}{3}$

12. $\dfrac{7x - 4}{-91x^2 + 108x - 32} \div \dfrac{x^2 + 4x - 5}{13x^2 + 109x - 72}$

_____

_____

Solve.

13. The formula for the volume of a cylinder is $\pi r^2 h$ and the formula for its
surface area is $2\pi r^2 + 2\pi rh$, where r is the radius and h is the height.
A cylindrical industrial storage tank has a surface area-to-volume ratio
of 3. If the height of the cylindrical tank is 2 meters, what is the radius?

_____

LESSON 9-3 Solving Rational Equations

Practice and Problem Solving: A/B

Identify any excluded values. Rewrite the equation with 0 on one side. Then graph to find the solution.

1. $-\dfrac{2}{x-3}=2$

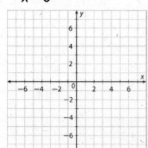

2. $\dfrac{4}{x-2}=-2$

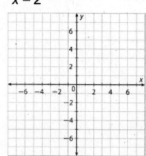

_____   _____

Find the LCD for each pair.

3. $\dfrac{13}{4x}$ and $\dfrac{27}{3x^2}$

4. $\dfrac{11}{x^2+3x+2}$ and $\dfrac{1}{x+2}$

_____   _____

Solve each equation algebraically.

5. $\dfrac{1}{x}-\dfrac{x-2}{3x}=\dfrac{4}{3x}$

6. $\dfrac{5x-5}{x^2-4x}-\dfrac{5}{x^2-4x}=\dfrac{1}{x}$

_____   _____

7. $\dfrac{x^2-7x+10}{x}+\dfrac{1}{x}=x+4$

8. $\dfrac{4}{x^2-4}=\dfrac{1}{x-2}$

_____   _____

Solve.

9. The time required to deliver and install a computer at a customer's location is $t=4+\dfrac{d}{r}$, where t is time in hours, d is the distance, in miles, from the warehouse to the customer's location, and r is the average speed of the delivery truck. If it takes 6.2 hours for the employee to deliver and install a computer for a customer located 100 miles from the warehouse, what is the average speed of the delivery truck?

_____

LESSON 9-3

Solving Rational Equations
Practice and Problem Solving: C

Identify any excluded values. Rewrite the equation with 0 on one side. Then graph to find the solution.

1. $12 = \dfrac{2}{x-3} + 14$

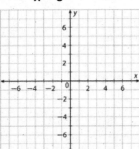

_____

2. $\dfrac{3}{x-1} - 16 = -16$

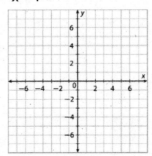

_____

Find the LCD for each pair.

3. $\dfrac{7}{3x^2y^6}$ and $\dfrac{23}{5x^3y^2}$

_____

4. $\dfrac{17}{x^2+x-2}$ and $\dfrac{5x}{x^2-x-6}$

_____

Solve each equation algebraically.

5. $-\dfrac{6}{x} + 1 = \dfrac{7}{x^2}$

_____

6. $\dfrac{4x}{x-4} = \dfrac{2x+8}{x-4}$

_____

7. $1 + \dfrac{x}{x+3} = \dfrac{x^2-8x+12}{2x^2+13x+21}$

_____

8. $\dfrac{x^2+7x+10}{5x-30} + \dfrac{x}{x-6} = \dfrac{x^2-13x+40}{5x-30}$

_____

Solve.

9. An artist is designing a picture frame whose length *l* and width *w* satisfy the Golden Ratio, which is $\dfrac{w}{l} = \dfrac{l}{l+w}$. If the length of the frame is 24 inches, what is the width of the frame?

_____

LESSON 10-1

Inverses of Simple Quadratic and Cubic Functions

Practice and Problem Solving: A/B

Graph the function $f(x)$ for the domain $x \geq 0$. Then graph its inverse, $f^{-1}(x)$, and write a rule for the inverse function.

1. $f(x) = 0.25x^2$

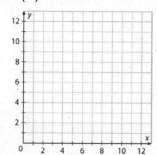

_____

2. $f(x) = x^2 + 3$

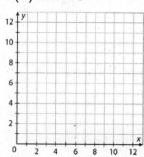

_____

Graph the function $f(x)$. Then graph its inverse, $f^{-1}(x)$, and write a rule for the inverse function.

3. $f(x) = 0.5x^3$

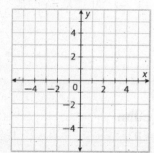

_____

4. $f(x) = x^3 - 2$

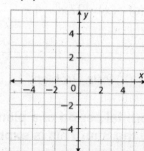

_____

The function $d = 4.9t^2$ gives the distance, d, in meters, that an object dropped from a height will fall in t seconds. Use this for Problems 5–6.

5. Express t as a function of d.

_____

_____

6. Find the number of seconds it takes an object to fall 150 feet. Round to the nearest tenth of a second.

_____

_____

Name _____ Date _____ Class_____

Inverses of Simple Quadratic and Cubic Functions

Practice and Problem Solving: C

Solve. Assume the domain is restricted to $\{x | x \geq 0\}$.

1. Find the inverse of $f(x) = \dfrac{1}{10}x^2$.

   _____

2. Find the inverse of $f(x) = 2x^2 - 7$.

   _____

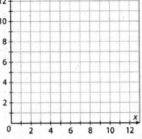

3. Graph $f(x)$ and $f^{-1}(x)$ from Problem 1.

Solve.

4. Find the inverse of $f(x) = 0.125x^3$.

   _____

5. Find the inverse of $f(x) = 27x^3 - 1$.

   _____

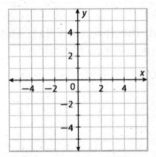

6. Graph $f(x)$ and $f^{-1}(x)$ from Problem 4.

The square of the orbital period of a planet is proportional to the cube of its distance from the Sun. This is expressed in the formula $T^2 = a^3$, where T is time, measured in years, and a is distance, measured in astronomical units (1 astronomical unit is the mean distance of Earth from the Sun). Use this information for Problems 7–9.

7. Express a as a function of T. Express T as a function of a.

   _____

8. Pluto's orbital period is approximately 247.9 times that of Earth's. Estimate Pluto's mean distance from the Sun. Show your work.

   _____

9. Venus's mean distance from the Sun is approximately 72.3% that of Earth's. Estimate Venus's orbital period. Show your work.

   _____

LESSON 10-2

Graphing Square Root Functions

Practice and Problem Solving: A/B

Graph each function, and identify its domain and range.

1. $f(x) = \sqrt{x - 4}$

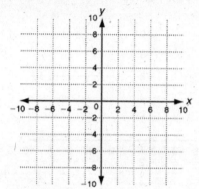

2. $f(x) = 2\sqrt{x} + 1$

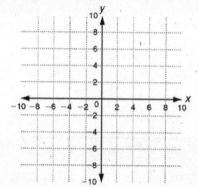

Domain: _____

Range: _____

Domain: _____

Range: _____

Using the graph of $f(x) = \sqrt{x}$ as a guide, describe the transformation.

3. $g(x) = 4\sqrt{x + 8}$ _____

4. $g(x) = -\sqrt{3x} + 2$ _____

Use the description to write the square root function g.

5. The parent function $f(x) = \sqrt{x}$ is reflected across the y-axis, vertically stretched by a factor of 7, and translated 3 units down.

6. The parent function $f(x) = \sqrt{x}$ is translated 2 units right, compressed horizontally by a factor of $\dfrac{1}{2}$, and reflected across the x-axis. _____

Solve.

7. The radius, r, of a cylinder can be found using the function $r = \sqrt{\dfrac{V}{\pi h}}$, where V is the volume and h is the height of the cylinder.

   a. Find the radius of a cylinder with a volume of 200 cubic inches and a height of 4 inches. Use $\pi = 3.14$. Round to the nearest hundredth. _____

   b. The volume of a cylinder is doubled without changing its height. How did its radius change? Explain your reasoning. _____

Name _____ Date _____ Class_____

Graphing Square Root Functions

Practice and Problem Solving: C

Graph each function, and identify its domain and range.

1. $g(x) = \dfrac{1}{2}\sqrt{-x} - 3$

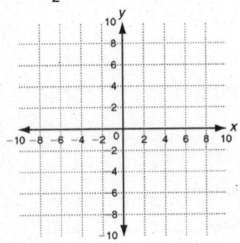

2. $g(x) = -4\sqrt{x+2} + 6$

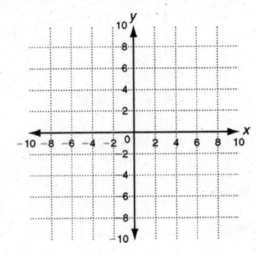

Domain: _____

Range: _____

Domain: _____

Range: _____

Use the description to write the square root function g.

3. The parent function $f(x) = \sqrt{x}$ is compressed vertically

by a factor of $\dfrac{1}{4}$, reflected across the x-axis, and

translated 6 units up. _____

4. The parent function $f(x) = \sqrt{x}$ is translated 8 units left,

reflected across the y-axis, and stretched horizontally

by a factor of 3. _____

Solve.

5. The frequency, *f*, in Hz, at which a simple pendulum rocks back and forth is given

by $f = \dfrac{1}{2\pi}\sqrt{\dfrac{g}{l}}$, where *g* is the strength of the gravitational field at the location

of the pendulum, and *l* is the length of the pendulum.

a. Find the frequency of a pendulum whose length
is 1 foot and where the gravitational field is
approximately 32 ft/s². _____

b. The strength of the gravitational field on the moon is

about $\dfrac{1}{6}$ as strong as on Earth. Find the frequency

of the same pendulum on the moon. _____

LESSON 10-3

Graphing Cube Root Functions

Practice and Problem Solving: A/B

Graph each cube root function. Then describe the graph as a transformation of the graph of the parent function. (The graph of the parent function is shown.)

1. $g(x) = \sqrt[3]{x-3} + 2$

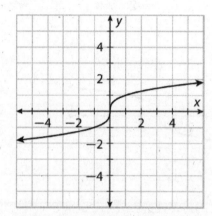

2. $g(x) = \frac{1}{2}\sqrt[3]{x+2} - 3$

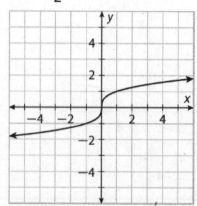

_____

Write the equation of the cube root function shown on the graph.
Use the form $g(x) = a\sqrt[3]{x-h} + k$.

3.

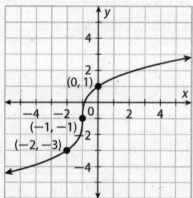

4.

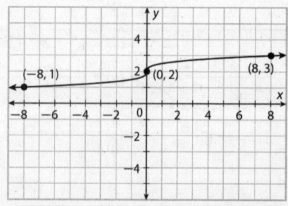

_____

Write an equation, $g(x)$, for the transformation equation described.

5. The graph of $f(x) = \sqrt[3]{x}$ is reflected across the y-axis and then translated 4 units down and 12 units to the left.

_____

6. The graph of $f(x) = \sqrt[3]{x}$ is stretched vertically by a factor of 8, reflected across the x-axis, and then translated 11 units to the right.

_____

LESSON
10-3

Graphing Cube Root Functions
Practice and Problem Solving: C

Graph each cube root function. Then describe the graph as a transformation of the graph of the parent function. (The graph of the parent function is shown.)

1. $g(x) = -2.5\sqrt[3]{x+2} + 1.5$

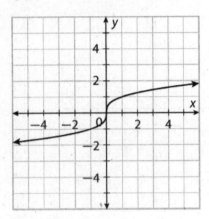

2. $g(x) = \sqrt[3]{-2x-4} - \dfrac{1}{2}$

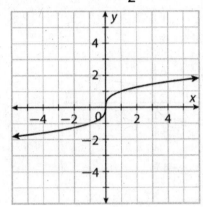

_____   _____

Write the equation of the cube root function shown on the graph.

3.

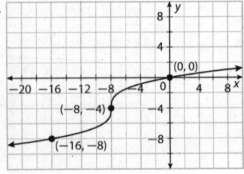

4.

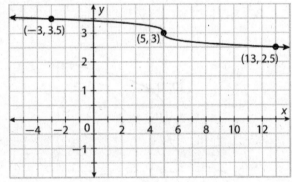

Write an equation, $g(x)$, for the transformation equation described.

5. The graph of the function $f(x) = 7\sqrt[3]{x-4} + 3$ is translated 2 units to the
left and then 4 units up.

_____

6. The graph of the function $f(x) = -\sqrt[3]{x+2} - 5$ is vertically stretched by a
factor of 3, translated 2 units to the right, and then reflected across the
x-axis.

_____

Radical Expressions and Rational Exponents
Practice and Problem Solving: A/B

Write each expression in radical form. Simplify numerical expressions when possible.

1. $64^{\frac{5}{6}}$

2. $(6x)^{\frac{3}{2}}$

3. $(-8)^{\frac{4}{3}}$

_____   _____   _____

4. $\left(5r^3\right)^{\frac{1}{4}}$

5. $27^{\frac{2}{3}}$

6. $(100a)^{\frac{1}{2}}$

_____   _____   _____

7. $10^{\frac{8}{5}}$

8. $\left(x^2\right)^{\frac{2}{5}}$

9. $(7x)^{-\frac{1}{3}}$

_____   _____   _____

Write each expression by using rational exponents. Simplify numerical expressions when possible.

10. $\left(\sqrt[4]{2}\right)^7$

11. $\left(\sqrt{5x}\right)^3$

12. $\sqrt[5]{51^4}$

_____   _____   _____

13. $\left(\sqrt{169}\right)^3$

14. $\left(\sqrt[4]{2v}\right)^3$

15. $\left(\sqrt[5]{n^2}\right)^2$

_____   _____   _____

16. $\dfrac{1}{\left(\sqrt{3m}\right)^3}$

17. $\sqrt[7]{36^{14}}$

18. $\dfrac{1}{\left(\sqrt[4]{5p}\right)^7}$

_____   _____   _____

Solve.

19. In every atom, electrons orbit the nucleus with a certain characteristic

velocity known as the Fermi-Thomas velocity, equal to $\dfrac{Z^{\frac{2}{3}}}{137}c$, where Z

is the number of protons in the nucleus and c is the speed of light. In
terms of c, what is the characteristic Fermi-Thomas velocity of the
electrons in Uranium, for which $Z = 92$?

_____

LESSON
11-1

Radical Expressions and Rational Exponents

Practice and Problem Solving: C

Write each expression in radical form. Simplify numerical expressions when possible.

1. $216^{\frac{2}{3}}$

2. $\left(121m^2\right)^{\frac{1}{3}}$

3. $\left(27x\right)^{\frac{5}{3}}$

_____ _____ _____

4. $\left(10b\right)^{2.5}$

5. $1000^{-\frac{2}{3}}$

6. $\left(37x^2\right)^{-\frac{1}{6}}$

_____ _____ _____

7. $\left(16x^3\right)^{\frac{3}{2}}$

8. $\left(5x\right)^{-1.25}$

9. $\left(162r^2\right)^{\frac{1}{4}}$

_____ _____ _____

Write each expression by using rational exponents. Simplify numerical expressions when possible.

10. $\left(\sqrt[19]{19n}\right)^2$

11. $\sqrt[5]{\left(3^5 x\right)^3}$

12. $\left(\sqrt[4]{181x^4}\right)^3$

_____ _____ _____

13. $\dfrac{1}{\left(\sqrt{5n}\right)^5}$

14. $\left(\sqrt{4x^3y^5}\right)^3$

15. $\left(\sqrt[5]{-6}\right)^3$

_____ _____ _____

16. $\left(\sqrt[3]{27x^3y^6}\right)^2$

17. $\sqrt[4]{30x^3}$

18. $\dfrac{1}{\left(\sqrt[3]{8a}\right)^5}$

_____ _____ _____

Solve.

19. Each key on a piano produces a frequency that is $2^{\frac{1}{12}}$ times higher than the frequency of the key immediately to its left. Moving n keys to the right of any key increases the frequency of the starting note by a factor $2^{\frac{n}{12}}$. The key corresponding to Concert A has a frequency of 440 Hz. What is the frequency of note D, which is 5 keys to the right of Concert A?

_____

LESSON 11-2

Simplifying Radical Expressions

Practice and Problem Solving: A/B

Simplify each expression. Assume all variables are positive.

1. $-3\sqrt{12r}$

_____

2. $4^{\frac{3}{2}} \cdot 4^{\frac{5}{2}}$

_____

3. $\dfrac{27^{\frac{4}{3}}}{27^{\frac{2}{3}}}$

_____

4. $\dfrac{\left(a^2\right)^2}{a^{\frac{3}{2}}b^{\frac{1}{2}} \cdot b}$

_____

5. $(27 \cdot 64)^{\frac{2}{3}}$

_____

6. $\left(\dfrac{1}{243}\right)^{\frac{1}{5}}$

_____

7. $\dfrac{(25x)^{\frac{3}{2}}}{5x^{\frac{1}{2}}}$

_____

8. $(4x)^{-\frac{1}{2}} \cdot (9x)^{\frac{1}{2}}$

_____

9. $3\sqrt[3]{81x^4y^2}$

_____

10. $-5\sqrt[3]{-500x^5y^3}$

_____

Solve.

11. The frequency, f, in Hz, at which a simple pendulum rocks back and

forth is given by $f = \dfrac{1}{2\pi}\sqrt{\dfrac{g}{l}}$, where g is the strength of the gravitational

field at the location of the pendulum, and l is the length of the pendulum.

a. Rewrite the formula so that it gives the length l of the pendulum in terms of g and f. Then simplify the formula using the fact that the gravitational field is approximately 32 ft/s².

_____

b. Use the equation found in part a to find the length of a pendulum, to the nearest foot, that has a frequency of 0.52 Hz.

_____

LESSON
11-2
Simplifying Radical Expressions
Practice and Problem Solving: C

Simplify each expression. Assume all variables are positive.

1. $\left(x^{\frac{1}{2}} \cdot x^{\frac{1}{2}} y^{\frac{3}{2}}\right)^2$

2. $\left(\left(r^{\frac{7}{4}}\right)^{\frac{1}{4}} \cdot r\right)^2$

_____

3. $\left(\dfrac{x^8}{y^4}\right)^{\frac{3}{4}}$

4. $\left(\dfrac{x^3}{125}\right)^{\frac{1}{3}}$

_____

5. $\left(-8x^{18}\right)^{\frac{2}{3}}\left(\sqrt[3]{y^6}\right)$

6. $\dfrac{x^{-2}y^2 \cdot y^2}{\left(x^{-\frac{1}{2}}\right)^{-\frac{1}{2}} \cdot \left(x^{-1}y^{-2}\right)^{-1}}$

_____

7. $\left(\sqrt[3]{-8x^9}\right)^2$

8. $(3x)^{\frac{2}{3}}(3x)^{\frac{7}{3}}$

_____

9. $\left(\dfrac{m^8}{n^{12}}\right)^{-\frac{1}{4}}$

10. $5\sqrt[3]{-750u^5v^5}$

_____

Solve.

11. Rafael is renting a cube-shaped bounce house for a party. The area in his yard he has marked off for the bounce house is 462.25 square feet.

   a. The rental company is able to provide Rafael with volumes of its various bounce houses. Rafael wants to know the area of a side. Use rational exponents to write a formula that Rafael could use to find the area of one side of the bounce house given its volume.

_____

   b. The bounce house Rafael likes best has a volume of 9261 ft³. What area of ground will the bounce house cover in square feet? Will the bounce house fit in the spot he has marked off? Show your work.

_____

Solving Radical Equations

Practice and Problem Solving: A/B

Solve each equation.

1. $\sqrt{x+6} = 7$

_____

2. $\sqrt{5x} = 10$

_____

3. $\sqrt{2x+5} = \sqrt{3x-1}$

_____

4. $\sqrt{x+4} = 3\sqrt{x}$

_____

5. $\sqrt[3]{x-6} = \sqrt[3]{3x+24}$

_____

6. $3\sqrt[3]{x} = \sqrt[3]{7x+5}$

_____

7. $\sqrt{-14x+2} = x-3$

_____

8. $(x+4)^{\frac{1}{2}} = 6$

_____

9. $4(x-3)^{\frac{1}{2}} = 8$

_____

10. $4(x-12)^{\frac{1}{3}} = -16$

_____

11. $\sqrt{3x+6} = 3$

_____

12. $\sqrt{x-4} + 3 = 9$

_____

13. $\sqrt{x+7} = \sqrt{2x-1}$

_____

14. $\sqrt{2x-7} = 2x$

_____

Solve.

15. A biologist is studying two species of animals in a habitat. The population,

p_1, of one of the species is growing according to $p_1 = 500t^{\frac{3}{2}}$ and the

population, p_2, of the other species is growing according to $p_2 = 100t^2$,
where time, t, is measured in years. After how many years will the
populations of the two species be equal?

_____

LESSON 11-3

Solving Radical Equations

Practice and Problem Solving: C

Solve each equation.

1. $\sqrt[3]{4x+1} - 5 = 0$

2. $3\sqrt{x-11} = 18$

_____

_____

3. $\sqrt[4]{10x+11} = 3$

4. $\sqrt[3]{3x} = \sqrt[3]{2x+9}$

_____

_____

5. $x + 2 = \sqrt{3x+6}$

6. $(10x-25)^{\frac{1}{2}} = x$

_____

_____

7. $5(6x+1)^{\frac{1}{4}} = 10$

8. $4(7x+18)^{\frac{1}{2}} = 4x$

_____

_____

9. $\sqrt{4x+5} = 3$

10. $\sqrt[3]{x+3} = 2$

_____

_____

11. $\sqrt{x-7} + 9 = 12$

12. $\sqrt[3]{x-6} + 7 = 4$

_____

_____

13. $\sqrt{3x-1} = \sqrt{x+7}$

14. $\sqrt[3]{x+2} - 1 = 4$

_____

_____

Solve.

15. Einstein's theory of relativity states that the mass of an object increases as the object's velocity increases. The mass, $m(v)$, of an object traveling with velocity, v, is given by $m(v) = \dfrac{m_0}{\sqrt{1 - \dfrac{v^2}{c^2}}}$, where c is the speed of light and m_0 is the mass of the object at rest. In terms of c, solve for the velocity at which the effective mass, $m(v)$, of the particle has increased to twice its mass at rest, m_0.

_____

LESSON 12-1 Arithmetic Sequences

Practice and Problem Solving: A/B

Write an explicit rule and a recursive rule for each sequence.

1.

n	1	2	3	4	5
$f(n)$	8	12	16	20	24

_____

_____

2.

n	1	2	3	4	5
$f(n)$	11	7	3	−1	−5

_____

_____

3.

n	1	2	3	4	5
$f(n)$	−20	−13	−6	1	8

_____

_____

4.

n	1	2	3	4	5
$f(n)$	2.7	4.3	5.9	7.5	9.1

_____

_____

5.

n	1	2	3	4	5
$f(n)$	1	−8	−17	−26	−35

_____

_____

6.

n	1	2	3	4	5
$f(n)$	−3	2.5	8	13.5	19

_____

_____

Solve.

7. The explicit rule for an arithmetic sequence is $f(n) = 13 + 6(n - 1)$.
   Find the first four terms of the sequence.

   _____

8. Helene paid back $100 in Month 1 of her loan. In each month after
   that, she paid back $50. Write an explicit formula and a recursive
   formula that shows $f(n)$, the total amount Helene had paid back by
   Month n.

   _____

9. The explicit rule for an arithmetic sequence is $f(n) = 18 + 5(n - 1)$.
   Write a recursive rule for this sequence.

   _____

10. A recursive rule for an arithmetic sequence is $f(1) = 7$, $f(n) = f(n - 1) + 47$ for $n \geq 2$. Write an explicit rule for this sequence.

   _____

LESSON
12-1

Arithmetic Sequences

Practice and Problem Solving: C

Write an explicit rule and a recursive rule for each sequence.

1.

n	1	2	3	4	5
$f(n)$	−3.4	−2.1	−0.8	0.5	1.8

_____

_____

2.

n	1	2	3	4	5
$f(n)$	$\frac{1}{6}$	$\frac{1}{4}$	$\frac{1}{3}$	$\frac{5}{12}$	$\frac{1}{2}$

_____

_____

3.

n	1	3	5	6	9
$f(n)$	82	81	80	79.5	78

_____

_____

4.

n	1	4	8	13	19
$f(n)$	−22	2	34	74	122

_____

_____

Solve.

5. A recursive rule for an arithmetic sequence is $f(1) = -8$, $f(n) = f(n - 1) - 6.5$ for $n \geq 2$. Write an explicit rule for this sequence.

_____

6. The third and thirtieth terms of an arithmetic sequence are 4 and 85. Write an explicit rule for this sequence.

_____

7. $f(n) = 900 - 60(n - 1)$ represents the amount Oscar still needs to repay on a loan at the beginning of Month n. Find the amount Oscar pays monthly and the month in which he will make his last payment.

_____

8. Find the first six terms of the sequence whose explicit formula is $f(n) = (-1)^n$. Explain whether it is an arithmetic sequence.

_____

9. An arithmetic sequence has common difference of 5.6, and its tenth term is 75. Write a recursive formula for this sequence.

_____

10. The cost of a college's annual tuition follows an arithmetic sequence. The cost was $35,000 in 2010 and $40,000 in 2012. According to this sequence, what will tuition be in 2020?

_____

Geometric Sequences

Practice and Problem Solving: A/B

Each rule represents a geometric sequence. If the given rule is recursive, write it as an explicit rule. If the rule is explicit, write it as a recursive rule. Assume that $f(1)$ is the first term of the sequence.

1. $f(n) = 11(2)^{n-1}$

2. $f(1) = 2.5$; $f(n) = f(n-1) \cdot 3.5$ for $n \geq 2$

_____

_____

3. $f(1) = 27$; $f(n) = f(n-1) \cdot \dfrac{1}{3}$ for $n \geq 2$

4. $f(n) = -4(0.5)^{n-1}$

_____

_____

Write an explicit rule for each geometric sequence based on the given terms from the sequence. Assume that the common ratio r is positive.

5. $a_1 = 90$ and $a_2 = 360$

6. $a_1 = 16$ and $a_3 = 4$

_____

_____

7. $a_1 = 2$ and $a_5 = 162$

8. $a_2 = 30$ and $a_3 = 10$

_____

_____

9. $a_4 = 135$ and $a_5 = 405$

10. $a_3 = 400$ and $a_5 = 256$

_____

_____

11. $a_2 = 80$ and $a_5 = 10$

12. $a_4 = 22$ and $a_7 = 0.022$

_____

_____

A bank account earns a constant rate of interest each month. The account was opened on March 1 with $18,000 in it. On April 1, the balance in the account was $18,045. Use this information for Problems 13–15.

13. Write an explicit rule and a recursive rule that can be used to find $A(n)$, the balance after n months.

_____

14. Find the balance after 5 months.

_____

15. Find the balance after 5 years.

_____

Geometric Sequences

Practice and Problem Solving: C

Each rule represents a geometric sequence. If the given rule is recursive, write it as an explicit rule. If the rule is explicit, write it as a recursive rule. Assume that f(1) is the first term of the sequence.

1. $f(1) = \dfrac{2}{3}$; $f(n) = f(n-1) \cdot 8$ for $n \geq 2$

2. $f(n) = -10(0.4)^{n-1}$

_____   _____

Write an explicit rule for each geometric sequence based on the given terms from the sequence. Assume that the common ratio *r* is positive.

3. $a_1 = 6$ and $a_4 = 162$

4. $a_2 = 9$ and $a_4 = 2.25$

_____   _____

5. $a_4 = 0.01$ and $a_5 = 0.0001$

6. $a_3 = \dfrac{1}{48}$ and $a_4 = \dfrac{1}{192}$

_____   _____

7. $a_3 = 32$ and $a_6 = \dfrac{256}{125}$

8. $a_2 = -4$ and $a_4 = -9$

_____   _____

Solve.

9. A geometric sequence contains the terms $a_3 = 40$ and $a_5 = 640$.
   Write the explicit rules for $r > 0$ and for $r < 0$.

   _____

10. The sum of the first *n* terms of the geometric sequence $f(n) = ar^{n-1}$ can
    be found using the formula $\dfrac{a(r^n - 1)}{r - 1}$. Use this formula to find the sum
    $1 + 3 + 3^2 + 3^3 + ... + 3^{10}$. Check your answer the long way.

    _____

11. An account earning interest compounded annually was worth $44,100
    after 2 years and $48,620.25 after 4 years. What is the interest rate?

    _____

12. There are 64 teams in a basketball tournament. All teams play in the
    first round but only winning teams move on to subsequent rounds.
    Write an explicit rule for $T(n)$, the number of games in the *n*th round of
    the tournament. State the domain of the rule.

    _____

LESSON 12-3 Geometric Series
Practice and Problem Solving: A/B

Determine the values of *a*, *n*, and *r* for each geometric series. Then use the summation formula to find the sum.

1. $1 + 6 + 36 + 216 + 1296$

2. $2 - 12 + 72 - 432$

3. $-1 - 4 - 16 - 64 - 256$

4. $-4 + 8 - 16 + 32 - 64$

Determine the number of terms in each geometric series. Then evaluate the sum.

5. $3 + 15 + 75 + ... + 46,875$

6. $2 - 6 + 18 - ... + 1458$

7. $-1 - 5 - 25 - ... - 78,125$

8. $-4 - 16 - 64 - ... - 262,144$

Evaluate each geometric series described.

9. A geometric series begins with 4, ends with $\frac{1}{64}$, and has terms that decrease successively by half.

10. A geometric series has 9 terms, starts with –2, and has a common ratio of –4.

Solve.

11. Deanna received an e-mail asking her to forward it to 10 other people. Assume that no one breaks the chain and that there are no duplicate recipients. How many e-mails will have been sent after 8 generations, including Deanna's?

LESSON
12-3

Geometric Series

Practice and Problem Solving: C

Determine the values of *a*, *n*, and *r* for each geometric series. Then use the summation formula to find the sum.

1. $1.25 + 5 + 20 + 80 + 320$

_____

_____

2. $-2 + 10 - 50 + 250 - 1250$

_____

_____

3. $2 + 1 + \dfrac{1}{2} + \dfrac{1}{4}$

_____

_____

4. $-20 - 10 - 5 - \dfrac{5}{2} - \dfrac{5}{4}$

_____

_____

Evaluate the sum.

5. $-2.5 - 5 - 10 - \ldots - 160$

_____

6. $-64 + 32 - 16 + \ldots - 0.25$

_____

7. $1 - \dfrac{1}{4} + \dfrac{1}{16} - \ldots - \dfrac{1}{262,144}$

_____

8. $2 + 1 + \dfrac{1}{2} + \ldots + \dfrac{1}{256}$

_____

Evaluate each geometric series described.

9. A geometric series begins with –2, ends with $-\dfrac{4374}{78,125}$, and has terms that decrease successively by 40%.

_____

10. A geometric series has 9 terms that start with $-\dfrac{7}{5}$ and have a common ratio of $\dfrac{1}{2}$.

_____

Solve.

11. Miguel paid $9600 in rent for his apartment the first year. Every year for the next 3 years the rent increased 5%.

   a. How much rent did he pay in the fourth year? _____

   b. How much rent did he pay altogether in the 4 years? _____

Name _____ Date _____ Class_____

Exponential Growth Functions
Practice and Problem Solving: A/B

Use two points to write an equation for each function shown.

1.

x	0	1	2	3
f(x)	6	18	54	162

2.

x	−4	−2	0	2	4
f(x)	−2.98	−2.75	−2	1	13

_____   _____

Graph each function.

3. $y = 5(2)^x$

4. $y = -2(3)^x$

5. $y = \frac{1}{2}(2)^{x-1} + 3$

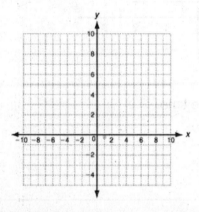
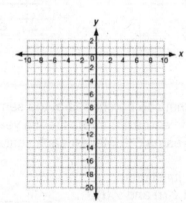
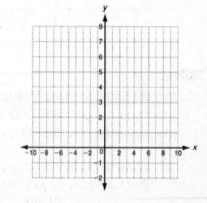

Solve.

6. The annual sales for a fast food restaurant are $650,000 and are increasing at a rate of 4% per year. Write the function $f(n)$ that expresses the annual sales after n years. Then find the annual sales after 5 years.

_____

7. Starting with 25 members, a club doubled its membership every year. Write the function $f(n)$ that expresses the number of members in the club after n years. Then find the number of members after 6 years.

_____

8. During a certain period of time, about 70 northern sea otters had an annual growth rate of 18%. Write the function $f(n)$ that expresses the population of sea otters after n years. Then find the population of sea otters after 4 years.

_____

LESSON
13-1

Exponential Growth Functions

Practice and Problem Solving: C

Graph each function. On your graph, include points to indicate the ordered pairs for $x = -1, 0, 1,$ and 2.

1. $f(x) = 0.75(2)^x$

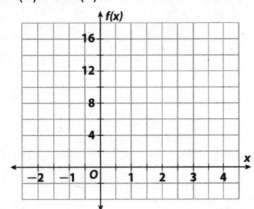

2. $f(x) = 6(3)^{x-1}$

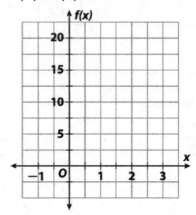

Solve.

3. Odette has two investments that she purchased at the same time. Investment 1 cost $10,000 and earns 4% interest each year. Investment 2 cost $8000 and earns 6% interest each year.

   a. Write exponential growth functions
      that could be used to find $v_1(t)$ and $v_2(t)$, _____

      the values of the investments after t years. _____

   b. Find the value of each investment after 5 years.
      Explain why the difference between their values, _____

      which was initially $2000, is now less. _____

4. If A is deposited in a bank account at r% annual interest, compounded annually, its value at the end of n years $V(n)$ can be found using the

   formula $V(n) = A\left(1 + \dfrac{r}{100}\right)^n$. Suppose that $5000 is invested in an

   account paying 4% interest. Find its value after 10 years.

   _____

5. The graph of $f(x) = 6(3)^{x-1}$ from Problem 2 moves closer and closer

   to the x-axis as x decreases. Does the graph ever reach the x-axis? Explain your reasoning and what your conclusion implies about the range of the function.

   _____

   _____

LESSON 13-2

Exponential Decay Functions
Practice and Problem Solving: A/B

Use two points to write an equation for each function shown.

1.

x	0	1	2	3
f(x)	36	27	20.25	15.1875

2.

x	−2	0	2	4
f(x)	84	21	5.25	1.3125

_____   _____

Graph each function.

3. $y = \left(\dfrac{1}{2}\right)^x - 3$

4. $y = -(0.5)^{x+3} - 3$

5. $y = 3\left(\dfrac{1}{2}\right)^x$

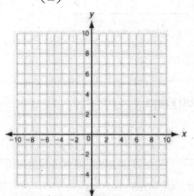   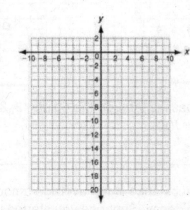   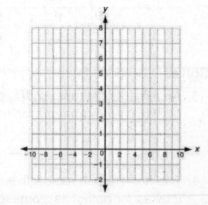

Solve.

6. If a basketball is bounced from a height of 15 feet, the function $f(x) = 15(0.75)^x$ gives the height of the ball in feet of each bounce, where x is the bounce number. What will be the height of the 5th bounce? Round to the nearest tenth of a foot.

_____

7. The value of a company's equipment is $25,000 and decreases at a rate of 15% per year. Write the function, $f(n)$, that expresses the value of the equipment after n years. Then find the value of the equipment in year eight.

_____

8. In 1995, the population of a town was 33,500. It is decreasing at a rate of 2.5% per decade. Write the function, $f(n)$, that expresses the population of the town after n decades. What is the expected population of the town in the year 2025 to the nearest hundred?

_____

LESSON
13-2

Exponential Decay Functions

Practice and Problem Solving: C

Graph each function. On your graph, include points to indicate the ordered pairs for $x = -1, 0, 1,$ and 2.

1. $f(x) = 5(0.4)^x + 1$

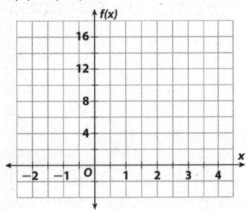

2. $f(x) = -15(0.3)^{x+1} + 20$

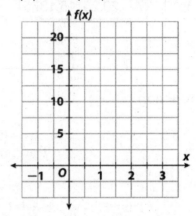

Solve.

3. An exponential function $f(x)$ passes through the points (2, 360) and (3, 216). Write an equation for $f(x)$.

_____

4. The half-life of a radioactive substance is the average amount of time it takes for half of its atoms to decay. Suppose you started with 200 grams of a substance with a half-life of 3 minutes. How many minutes have passed if 25 grams now remain? Explain your reasoning.

_____

_____

5. Colleen's office equipment is depreciating at a rate of 9% per year. She paid $24,500 for it in 2009. Write the function $f(n)$ that expresses the value of the equipment after n years. What will the equipment be worth in 2015 to the nearest hundred dollars?

_____

6. A car depreciates in value by 20% each year. Graham argued that the value of the car after 5 years must be $0, since 20% • 5 = 100%. Do you agree or disagree? Explain fully.

_____

_____

LESSON 13-3

The Base e

Practice and Problem Solving: A/B

Given the function of the form $g(x) = a \cdot e^{x-h} + k$,

  a. **Identify a, h, and k.**
  b. **Identify and plot the reference points.**
  c. **Draw the graph.**
  d. **State the domain and range in set notation.**

1. $g(x) = 2e^x - 4$ 2. $g(x) = e^{x-5} + 3$ 3. $g(x) = 0.5e^{x+4} - 1$

  a. _____   a. _____   a. _____

  b. _____   b. _____   b. _____

  c. 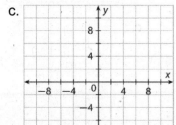   c. 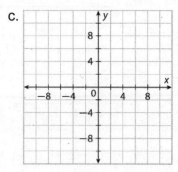   c.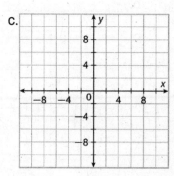

  d. _____   d. _____   d. _____

Solve.

4. When interest is compounded continuously, the amount A in an account after t years is found using the formula $A = Pe^{rt}$, where P is the amount of principal and r is the annual interest rate.

  a. Use the formula to compute the balance of an investment that had a principal amount of $4500 and earned 5% interest for 6 years.

     _____

  b. What is the amount of interest earned in the investment?

     _____

5. Use the natural decay function, $N(t) = N_0 e^{-kt}$, to find the decay constant, k, for a substance that has a half-life of 1000 years.

  _____

LESSON 13-3

The Base e

Practice and Problem Solving: C

Given the function of the form $g(x) = a \cdot e^{x-h} + k,$

   a. **Identify a, h, and k.**
   b. **Identify and plot the reference points.**
   c. **Draw the graph.**
   d. **State the domain and range in set notation.**

1. $g(x) = \dfrac{1}{5}e^{x-3} - 4$

   a. _____

   b. _____

   c.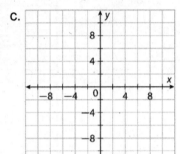

   d. _____

2. $g(x) = -4e^{x+2} + 6$

   a. _____

   b. _____

   c.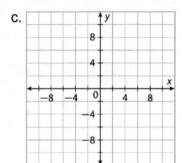

   d. _____

3. $g(x) = -0.75e^{x-5} + 2.5$

   a. _____

   b. _____

   c.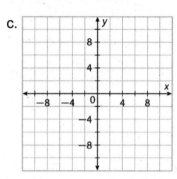

   d. _____

Solve.

4. When interest is compounded continuously, the amount A in an account after t years is found using the formula $A = Pe^{rt}$, where P is the amount of principal and r is the annual interest rate. Ariana has a choice of two investments that are both compounded continuously. She can invest \$12,000 at 5% for 8 years, or she can invest \$9000 at 6.5% for 7 years. Which investment will result in the greater amount of interest earned?

_____

5. Use the natural decay function, $N(t) = N_0 e^{-kt}$, to find the decay rate and the age of a fossil containing 35% of the original amount of a particular substance, given that the substance has a half-life of 2450 years.

_____

Name _____ Date _____ Class_____

Compound Interest

Practice and Problem Solving: A/B

For each investment described, (a) write an exponential growth model that represents the value of the account at any time *t*, and (b) use a graphing calculator to solve for *t* for the given value.

1. The principal amount, $6250, earns 4.25% interest compounded annually. How long will it take for the account's value to surpass $9500?

   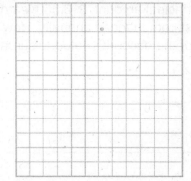

   a. _____

   b. _____

2. The principal amount, $4200, earns 3.6% interest compounded quarterly. How long will it take for the account's value to surpass $15,000?

   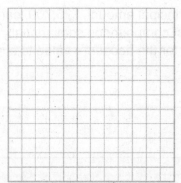

   a. _____

   b. _____

3. The principal amount, $13,000, earns 8.7% interest compounded continuously. How long will it take for the account's value to reach $80,000?

   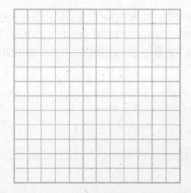

   a. _____

   b. _____

Solve.

4. Shiloh plans to make a deposit into one of the accounts shown in the table. He wants to choose the account with the highest effective interest rate, *R*.

	Account A	Account B
Nominal Interest Rate	4.25%	4.8%
Compounding Period	Monthly	Semiannually

   a. Find R_A and R_B.   _____

   b. Which account should he choose? _____

LESSON 13-4

Compound Interest

Practice and Problem Solving: C

For each investment described, (a) write an exponential growth model that represents the value of the account at any time *t*, and (b) use a graphing calculator to solve for *t* for the given value.

1. The principal amount, $16,550, earns 2.89% interest compounded annually. How long will it take for the account's value to surpass $75,250?

   a. _____

   b. _____

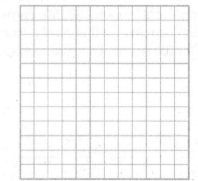

2. The principal amount, $25,700, earns 6.925% interest compounded semiannually. How long will it take for the account's value to surpass $150,000?

   a. _____

   b. _____

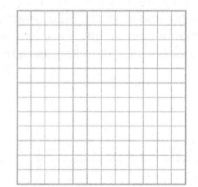

3. The principal amount, $123,500, earns 7.65% interest compounded continuously. How long will it take for the account's value to reach $300,000?

   a. _____

   b. _____

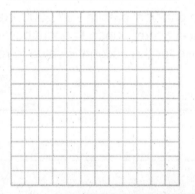

Solve.

4. Yolanda plans to make a deposit into one of the accounts shown in the table. She wants to choose the account with the lowest effective interest rate, *R*.

	Account A	Account B
Nominal Interest Rate	8.25%	8.16%
Compounding Period	Continuously	Monthly

   a. Find R_A and R_B. _____

   b. Which account should she choose? _____

Fitting Exponential Functions to Data
Practice and Problem Solving: A/B

Determine whether *f* is an exponential function of *x*. If so, find the constant ratio.

1.

x	−1	0	1	2	3
f(x)	9	3	1	0.3	0.9

_____

2.

x	−1	0	1	2	3
f(x)	0.01	0.03	0.15	0.87	5.19

_____

3.

x	−1	0	1	2	3
f(x)	$\frac{5}{6}$	$\frac{5}{2}$	7.5	22.5	67.5

_____

4.

x	−1	0	1	2	3
f(x)	1	0.5	0.33	0.25	0.2

_____

Use exponential regression to find a function that models the data.

5.

x	1	2	3	4	5
f(x)	14	7.1	3.4	1.8	0.8

_____

6.

x	2	12	22	32	42
f(x)	5	20	80	320	1280

_____

Solve.

7. a. Bernice is selling seashells she has found at the beach. The price of each shell depends on its length. Find an exponential model for the data.

Length of Shell (cm)	5	8	12	20	25
Price ($)	2	3.5	5	18	40

_____

b. What is the length of a shell selling for $9.00? _____

c. If Bernice found a 40 cm conch shell, how much could she sell it for? _____

8. a. Use exponential regression to find a function that models this data.

Time (years)	0	10	20	30	40
Population (thousands)	10.1	9.8	17.5	19.9	28.7

_____

b. When will the population exceed 50 thousand? _____

c. What will the population be after 100 years? _____

LESSON 14-1

Fitting Exponential Functions to Data

Practice and Problem Solving: C

Determine whether *f* is an exponential function of *x*. If so, find the constant ratio.

1.

x	−1	0	1	2	3
f(x)	3.28	8.4	14.8	22.8	32.8

_____

2.

x	−1	0	1	2	3
f(x)	3.5	7	14	21	28

_____

3.

x	−1	0	1	2	3
f(x)	$\frac{8}{3}$	4	6	9	$\frac{27}{2}$

_____

4.

x	−1	0	1	2	3
f(x)	$\frac{243}{4}$	$\frac{81}{2}$	27	18	12

_____

Use exponential regression to find a function that models the data.

5.

x	1	2	3	4	5
f(x)	9.3	21.8	50.8	118.6	276.6

_____

6.

x	2	4	6	8	10
f(x)	413.2	45.5	4.9	0.6	0.1

_____

7.

x	1	2	3	4	5
f(x)	11.3	8.4	6.3	4.7	3.6

_____

8.

x	2	4	6	8	10
f(x)	14.2	21.3	33.9	57.2	99.8

_____

Solve.

9. a. Use exponential regression to find a function that models this data.

Time (min)	1	3	6	8	10
Bacteria	413	575	945	1316	1832

_____

b. When will the number of bacteria reach 2500? _____

c. How many bacteria will exist after 1 hour? _____

LESSON 14-2 Choosing Among Linear, Quadratic, and Exponential Models

Practice and Problem Solving: A/B

The table below shows the total attendance at major league baseball games, at 10-year intervals since 1930. Use the table for the problems that follow. Round all answers to the nearest thousandth.

Major League Baseball Total Attendance (y), in millions, in years since 1930 (x)									
x	0	10	20	30	40	50	60	70	80
y	10.1	9.8	17.5	19.9	28.7	43.0	54.8	72.6	73.1

1. Use a graphing calculator to find a linear regression equation for this data.

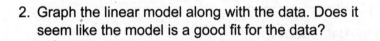

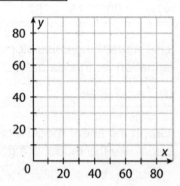

2. Graph the linear model along with the data. Does it seem like the model is a good fit for the data?

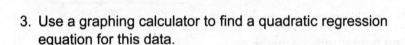

3. Use a graphing calculator to find a quadratic regression equation for this data.

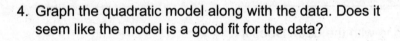

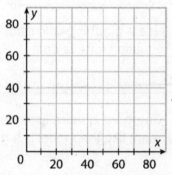

4. Graph the quadratic model along with the data. Does it seem like the model is a good fit for the data?

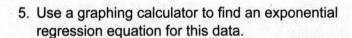

5. Use a graphing calculator to find an exponential regression equation for this data.

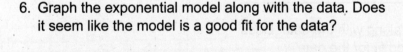

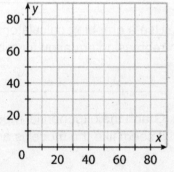

6. Graph the exponential model along with the data. Does it seem like the model is a good fit for the data?

_____

7. Use the exponential regression equation to predict major league baseball attendance in 2020. Based on the pattern of data, do you think this is a reasonable prediction? Explain.

_____

_____

Choosing Among Linear, Quadratic, and Exponential Models

LESSON
14-2

Practice and Problem Solving: C

A pot of boiling water is allowed to cool for 50 minutes. The table below shows the temperature of the water as it cools. Use the table for the problems that follow. Round all answers to the nearest thousandth.

Temperature of Water (y), in degrees Celsius, after cooling for x minutes										
x	0	5	10	15	20	25	30	35	40	45	50
y	100	75	57	44	34	26	21	17	14	11	10

1. Use a graphing calculator to find a linear regression equation for this data.

   _____

2. Graph the linear model along with the data. Does it seem like the model is a good fit for the data?

   _____

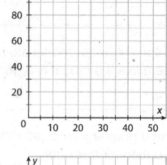

3. Use a graphing calculator to find a quadratic regression equation for this data.

   _____

4. Graph the quadratic model along with the data. Does it seem like the model is a good fit for the data?

   _____

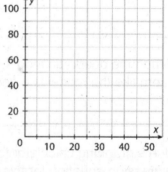

5. Use a graphing calculator to find an exponential regression equation for this data.

   _____

6. Graph the exponential model along with the data. Does it seem like the model is a good fit for the data?

   _____

7. Use each regression model to estimate the temperature of the water after 55 minutes. Which estimation seems the most likely?

   _____

LESSON 15-1 Defining and Evaluating a Logarithmic Function

Practice and Problem Solving: A/B

Write each exponential equation in logarithmic form.

1. $3^7 = 2187$

2. $12^2 = 144$

3. $5^3 = 125$

_____   _____   _____

Write each logarithmic equation in exponential form.

4. $\log_{10} 100{,}000 = 5$

5. $\log_4 1024 = 5$

6. $\log_9 729 = 3$

_____   _____   _____

Evaluate each expression without using a calculator.

7. $\log 1{,}000{,}000$

8. $\log 10$

9. $\log 1$

_____   _____   _____

10. $\log_4 16$

11. $\log_8 1$

12. $\log_5 625$

_____   _____   _____

Use the given x-values to graph each function. Then graph its inverse. Write an equation for the inverse function and describe its domain and range.

13. $f(x) = 2^x$; $x = -2, -1, 0, 1, 2, 3, 4$

14. $f(x) = \left(\dfrac{1}{2}\right)^x$; $x = -3, -2, -1, 0, 1, 2, 3$

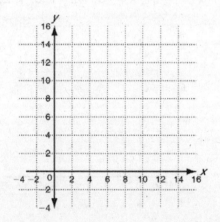

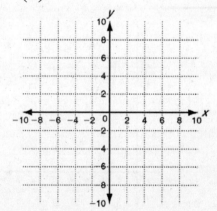

_____   _____

Solve.

15. The acidity level, or pH, of a liquid is given by the formula $pH = \log \dfrac{1}{[H^+]}$,

where $[H^+]$ is the concentration (in moles per liter) of hydrogen ions in the liquid. The hydrogen ion concentration in moles per liter for a certain brand of tomato vegetable juice is 0.000316.

   a. Write a logarithmic equation for the pH of the juice. _____

   b. What is the pH of the juice? _____

Name _____ Date _____ Class_____

Defining and Evaluating a Logarithmic Function
Practice and Problem Solving: C

Write each exponential equation in logarithmic form.

1. $20^3 = 8000$ 2. $11^4 = 14{,}641$ 3. $a^b = c$

_____   _____   _____

Write each logarithmic equation in exponential form.

4. $\log_{10} 10{,}000{,}000 = 7$ 5. $\log_6 216 = 3$ 6. $\log_p q = r$

_____   _____   _____

Evaluate each expression without using a calculator.

7. $\log 1$ 8. $\log 10{,}000$ 9. $\log 1000$

_____   _____   _____

10. $\log_5 3125$ 11. $\log_{15} 1$ 12. $\log_4 256$

_____   _____   _____

Use the given *x*-values to graph each function. Then graph its inverse. Write an equation for the inverse function and describe its domain and range.

13. $f(x) = 0.1^x$; $x = -1, 0, 1, 2$ 14. $f(x) = \left(\dfrac{5}{2}\right)^x$; $x = -3, -2, -1, 0, 1, 2, 3$

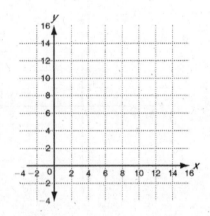   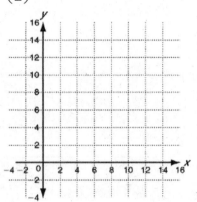

_____   _____

Solve.

15. The acidity level, or pH, of a liquid is given by the formula $\text{pH} = \log \dfrac{1}{[\text{H}^+]}$,

   where $[\text{H}^+]$ is the concentration (in moles per liter) of hydrogen ions in the liquid. The hydrogen ion concentration in moles per liter of a certain solvent is 0.00794.

   a. Write a logarithmic equation for the pH of the solvent. _____

   b. What is the pH of the solvent? _____

LESSON
15-2
Graphing Logarithmic Functions
Practice and Problem Solving: A/B

Graph each function. Find the asymptote. Tell how the graph is transformed from the graph of its parent function.

1. $f(x) = \log_2 x + 4$

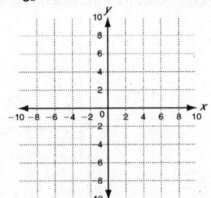

2. $f(x) = 3\log_4 (x + 6)$

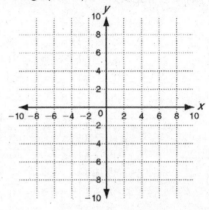

3. $f(x) = \log (x + 5)$

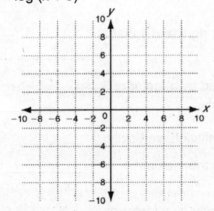

4. $f(x) = 3 + \ln x$

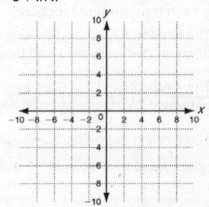

Write each transformed function.

5. The function $f(x) = \log (x + 1)$ is reflected across the *x*-axis and translated down 4 units.

_____

6. The function $f(x) = \log_8 (x - 3)$ is compressed vertically by a factor of $\frac{2}{5}$ and translated up 11 units.

_____

Solve.

7. The function $A(t) = Pe^{rt}$ is used to calculate the balance, *A*, of an investment in which the interest is compounded continuously at an annual rate, *r*, over *t* years. Find the inverse of the formula. Describe what information the inverse gives.

LESSON
15-2

Graphing Logarithmic Functions

Practice and Problem Solving: C

Graph each function. Find the asymptote. Tell how the graph is transformed from the graph of the parent function.

1. $f(x) = 2.5\log_2(x + 7) - 3$

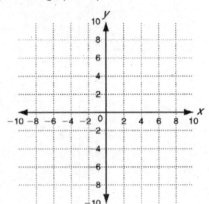

2. $f(x) = -0.8\ln(x - 1.5) + 2$

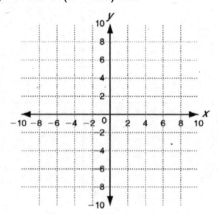

_____   _____

Write each transformed function.

3. The function $f(x) = -\log_9(x + 4)$ is translated 4 units right and 1 unit down and vertically stretched by a factor of 7.   _____

4. The function $f(x) = 3\ln(2x + 8)$ is vertically stretched by a factor of 3, translated 7 units up, and reflected across the *x*-axis.   _____

5. The function $f(x) = -\log(5 - x) - 2$ is translated 6 units left, vertically compressed by a factor of $\frac{1}{3}$, and reflected across the *x*-axis.   _____

6. The function $f(x) = 8\log_7 x - 5$ is compressed vertically by a factor of 0.5, translated right 1 unit, and reflected across the *x*-axis.   _____

7. What transformations does the function $f(x) = -\ln(x + 1) - 2$ undergo to become the function $g(x) = \ln(x - 1)$?   _____

Solve.

8. The function $A(t) = Pe^{rt}$ is used to calculate the balance, *A*, of an investment where the interest is compounded continuously at an annual rate, *r*, over *t* years. Find the inverse of the formula. Then use it to determine the amount of time it will take a $27,650 investment at 3.95% to reach a balance of $50,000.

_____

Name _____ Date _____ Class_____

LESSON
16-1

Properties of Logarithms
Practice and Problem Solving: A/B

Express as a single logarithm. Simplify, if possible.

1. $\log_3 9 + \log_3 27$

2. $\log_2 8 + \log_2 16$

3. $\log_{10} 80 + \log_{10} 125$

_____ _____ _____

4. $\log_6 8 + \log_6 27$

5. $\log_3 6 + \log_3 13.5$

6. $\log_4 32 + \log_4 128$

_____ _____ _____

Express as a single logarithm. Simplify, if possible.

7. $\log_2 80 - \log_2 10$

8. $\log_{10} 4000 - \log_{10} 40$

9. $\log_4 384 - \log_4 6$

_____ _____ _____

10. $\log_2 1920 - \log_2 30$

11. $\log_3 486 - \log_3 2$

12. $\log_6 180 - \log_6 5$

_____ _____ _____

Simplify, if possible.

13. $\log_4 4^6$

14. $\log_5 5^{x-5}$

15. $7^{\log_7 30}$

_____ _____ _____

16. $12^{\log_{12} 1}$

17. $\log_8 8^5$

18. $\log_3 9^4$

_____ _____ _____

Evaluate. Round to the nearest hundredth.

19. $\log_{12} 1$

20. $\log_3 30$

21. $\log_5 10$

_____ _____ _____

Solve.

22. The Richter magnitude of an earthquake, M, is related to the energy released in ergs, E, by the formula $M = \frac{2}{3}\log\left(\frac{E}{10^{11.8}}\right)$.

Find the energy released by an earthquake of magnitude 4.2. _____

Original content Copyright © by Houghton Mifflin Harcourt. Additions and changes to the original content are the responsibility of the instructor.

101

LESSON
16-1

Properties of Logarithms
Practice and Problem Solving: C

Express as a single logarithm. Simplify, if possible.

1. $\log_6 12 + \log_6 18$

   _____

2. $\log_3 81 - \log_3 27$

   _____

3. $\log_4 128 - \log_4 8$

   _____

4. $\log_6 18 + \log_6 72$

   _____

5. $\log_5 3125 - \log_5 25$

   _____

6. $\log_8 128 + \log_8 256$

   _____

7. $\log_5 5 + \log_5 125$

   _____

8. $\log_2 256 - \log_2 64$

   _____

9. $\log_3 8019 - \log_3 99$

   _____

10. $\log_8 80 + \log_8 51.2$

    _____

11. $\log_7 13.3 - \log_7 1.9$

    _____

12. $\log_{10} 125 + \log_{10} 80$

    _____

Evaluate. Round to the nearest hundredth.

13. $\log_8 8^6$

    _____

14. $2^{\log_2 8^x}$

    _____

15. $\log_2 16^5$

    _____

16. $\log_3 3^{(2x + 1)}$

    _____

17. $\log_4 16^{(x - 1)}$

    _____

18. $5^{\log_5 17}$

    _____

19. $\log_3 5^2$

    _____

20. $\log_5 \left(\dfrac{1}{125}\right)^2$

    _____

21. $\log_6 \left(\dfrac{1}{6^4}\right)^3$

    _____

22. $\log_4 20^2$

    _____

23. $\log_9 27^4$

    _____

24. $\log_2 10$

    _____

Solve.

25. Carmen has a painting presently valued at $5000. An art dealer told
    her the painting would appreciate at a rate of 6% per year. In how
    many years will the painting be worth $8000?

    a. Write a logarithmic expression representing the situation.   _____

    b. Simplify your expression. How many years will it take?   _____

LESSON 16-2

Solving Exponential Equations

Practice and Problem Solving: A/B

Solve each equation by graphing. If necessary, round to the nearest thousandth.

1. $5e^{x-3} = 75$

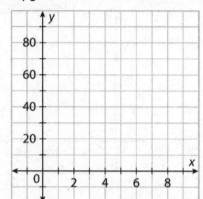

2. $8e^{-8x} + 8 = 17$

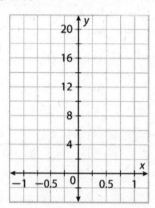

_____   _____

Solve each equation algebraically. If necessary, round to the nearest thousandth.

3. $5^{2x} = 20$ 4. $12^{2x-8} = 15$ 5. $2^{x+6} = 4$

_____   _____   _____

6. $16^{5x} = 64^{x+7}$ 7. $243^{0.2x} = 81^{x+5}$ 8. $25^{x} = 125^{x-2}$

_____   _____   _____

9. $\left(\dfrac{1}{2}\right)^{x} = 16^2$ 10. $\left(\dfrac{1}{32}\right)^{2x} = 64$ 11. $\left(\dfrac{1}{27}\right)^{x-6} = 27$

_____   _____   _____

12. $6e^{10x-8} - 4 = 34$ 13. $8(10)^{7x-6} - 8 = 59$ 14. $-6e^{-4x-1} + 3 = -37$

_____   _____   _____

Solve.

15. The population of a small farming community is declining at a rate of 7% per year. The decline can be expressed by the exponential equation $P = C(1 - 0.07)^t$, where P is the population after t years and C is the current population. If the population was 8500 in 2004, when will the population be less than 6000?

_____

**LESSON
16-2**

Solving Exponential Equations

Practice and Problem Solving: C

Solve each equation by graphing. If necessary, round to the nearest thousandth.

1. $e^{0.5x-9} + 0.2 = 73$

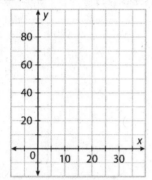

2. $9e^{x-7} - 5.5 = 51$

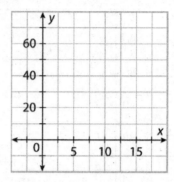

_____   _____

Solve each equation algebraically. If necessary, round to the nearest thousandth.

3. $16^{3x} = 8^{x+6}$

4. $3e^{2x-3} - 4 = 78$

5. $12^{x-1} = 20^2$

_____   _____   _____

6. $9^{2x} = 27^{x+4}$

7. $256^{0.5x} = 64^{2x+5}$

8. $216^{\frac{x}{3}} = 36^{2x+3}$

_____   _____   _____

9. $\left(\dfrac{1}{9}\right)^{3x} = 27$

10. $\left(\dfrac{1}{16}\right)^{x+5} = 8^2$

11. $\left(\dfrac{2}{5}\right)^{8x} = \left(\dfrac{25}{4}\right)^2$

_____   _____   _____

12. $-7(10)^{8-10x} + 9 = 4$

13. $-3(10)^{4-x} - 4 = -91$

14. $10e^{8x+1} - 3 = 70$

_____   _____   _____

Solve.

15. Lorena deposited $9000 into an account that earns 4.25% interest each year.

   a. Write an equation for the amount, A, in the account after t years. _____

   b. In how many years will her account exceed $20,000? _____

   c. If she waits for 50 years, how much will be in her account? _____

LESSON 17-1

Problem Solving with Trigonometry

Practice and Problem Solving: A/B

Use a calculator and inverse trigonometric ratios to find the unknown side lengths and angle measures. Round lengths to the nearest hundredth and angle measures to the nearest degree.

1.

2.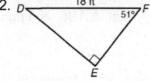

3.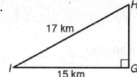

AC = _____   DE = _____   GH = _____

m∠B = _____   EF = _____   m∠H = _____

m∠C = _____   m∠D = _____   m∠I = _____

△XYZ has vertices X(6, 6), Y(6, 3), and Z(1, 3). Complete Problems 4–6 to find the side lengths to the nearest hundredth and the angle measures to the nearest degree.

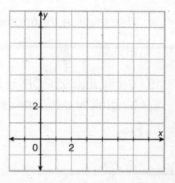

4. Plot the points and draw △XYZ.

5. Find XY and YZ from the graph. Use the Pythagorean Theorem to find XZ.

   XY = _____   YZ = _____   XZ = _____

6. Find the angle measures.

   m∠X _____   m∠Z _____

For each triangle, find all three side lengths to the nearest hundredth and all three angle measures to the nearest degree.

7. B(–2, –4), C(3, 3), D(–2, 3) _____

8. L(–1, –6), M(1, –6), N(–1, 1) _____

9. X(–4, 5), Y(–3, 5), Z(–3, 4) _____

Follow the steps to find the area of the triangle using trigonometry.

10. Draw a line from vertex U perpendicular to the base $\overline{TV}$ at a point W. Label its length h. Write the sine of ∠T as a ratio using variables in the figure. Solve for h. Then write the area of the triangle using your value for h.

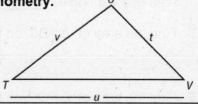

   sin T = ☐/☐   h = _____   Area = _____

   Area of a triangle = $\frac{1}{2}$ base × height

11. What is the area of the triangle if ∠T = 37°, u = 14, and v = 10? _____

LESSON 17-1

Problem Solving with Trigonometry

Practice and Problem Solving: C

For Problems 1–6, use trigonometry and the Pythagorean theorem to solve the right triangles on the coordinate plane. Show your work.

1. First use the slope formula to verify that $\triangle ABC$ is a right

   triangle. _____

2. Use the distance formula to find the length of each side.

   $AB =$ _____ $BC =$ _____ $AC =$ _____

3. Use the Pythagorean theorem to double check the side

   lengths. _____

4. Use inverse trigonometric ratios to find the acute angles.

   $m\angle A =$ _____ $m\angle C =$ _____

5. Verify that $\triangle PQR$ is a right triangle. Find the three side
   lengths and the measures of the acute angles.

   $PQ =$ _____ $QR =$ _____ $RP =$ _____

   $m\angle P =$ _____ $m\angle Q =$ _____

6. Find the side lengths and angle measures for $\triangle XYZ$,
   $X(1, 0)$, $Y(2, 1)$, $Z(5, -2)$.

   $XY =$ _____ $YZ =$ _____ $XZ =$ _____

   $m\angle X =$ _____ $m\angle Y =$ _____ $m\angle Z =$ _____

For Problems 7–10, use trigonometric functions to find the area of the triangles, to the nearest square unit.

7. If you know the lengths of two sides of any triangle, a and b, and
   the measure of the included angle, $m\angle C$, how can you find the

   area of the triangle? _____

8. Find the area of $\triangle ABC$ on the coordinate plane above.

   _____

9. Find the area of $\triangle PQR$ on the coordinate plane above.

   _____

10. Find the area of $\triangle XYZ$ in Problem 6 above. _____

LESSON 17-2

Law of Sines

Practice and Problem Solving: A/B

Find the measures indicated. Round to the nearest tenth.

1.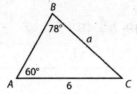

   a = _____   m∠C = _____

2.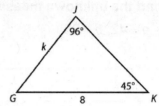

   k = _____   m∠G = _____

3.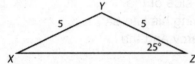

   m∠X = _____   m∠Y = _____

4.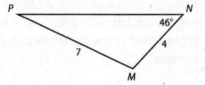

   m∠P = _____   m∠M = _____

5.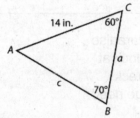

   c = ____ m∠A = ____ a = ____

6.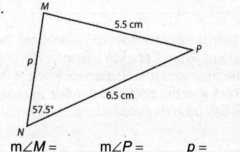

   m∠M = ____ m∠P = ____ p = ____

Determine how many triangles are possible and find the unknown measures. Round to the nearest tenth.

7. m∠B = 145°, a = 8, b = 22

_____

_____

8. m∠C = 75°, a = 8, c = 5

_____

_____

Law of Sines

Practice and Problem Solving: C

LESSON 17-2

Determine how many triangles are possible with the given measures and find the unknown measures.

1. $m\angle A = 107°$, $a = 42$, $b = 25$

2. $m\angle B = 65°$, $c = 19$, $b = 18$

_____

_____

_____

_____

_____

_____

3. Marcy flies her kite at a 45° angle from the ground. The kite string is approximately 235 feet long. Another person on the other side of the park tangles his kite with Marcy's. If the other person is flying his kite at a 72°angle, what is the approximate distance between Marcy and the other person?

_____

_____

_____

4. George sails his boat 3.7 miles from the dock at the mainland to Paradise Island. From Paradise Island, a 72° angle is formed between the dock at the mainland and Shipwreck Rock. If the distance between Shipwreck Rock and the dock is 5.6 miles, approximately how far does George need to sail from Paradise Island to reach Shipwreck Rock?

_____

_____

_____

LESSON 17-3

Law of Cosines

Practice and Problem Solving: A/B

Find the measures indicated. Round to the nearest tenth.

1.

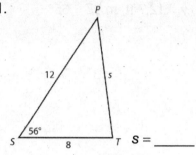

S = _____

2.

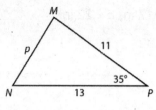

p = _____

3.

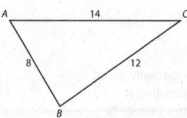

m∠A = _____ m∠B = _____ m∠C = _____

4.

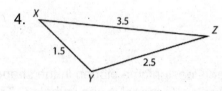

m∠X = _____ m∠Y = _____ m∠Z = _____

5.

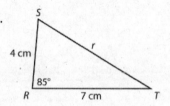

r = _____ m∠S = _____ m∠T = _____

6.

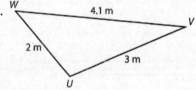

m∠W = _____ m∠U = _____ m∠V = _____

Determine whether there is enough information to use the Law of Cosines to solve for the triangle. Explain how you know.

7.

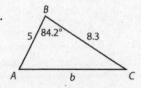

8.

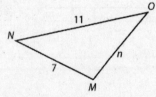

9.

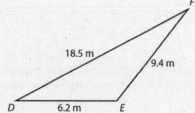

10.

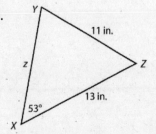

Name _____ Date _____ Class_____

Law of Cosines

Practice and Problem Solving: C

Solve each triangle. Round to the nearest tenth.

1. $a = 14$ in, $b = 17$ in, $c = 22$ in

2. $x = 9.2$ ft, $y = 12.7$ ft, $m\angle Z = 65°$

3. A farmer is designing a pigpen in the shape of a triangle. A partially completed scale model is shown below. The farmer estimates that it will cost $24 per yard for fencing. How much would it cost the farmer to build the entire fence?

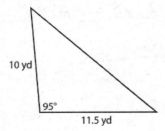

4. Solve for *x* using the figure below.

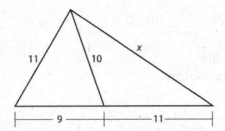

LESSON
18-1 **Angles of Rotation and Radian Measure**

Practice and Problem Solving: A/B

Draw an angle with the given measure in standard position.

1. −420°

2. 405°

3. −450°

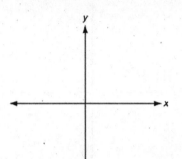
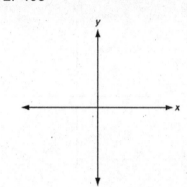
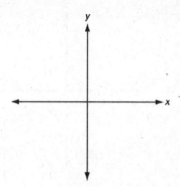

Find the measures of a positive angle and a negative angle that are coterminal with each given angle.

4. $\theta = 425°$

5. $\theta = -316°$

6. $\theta = -800°$

_____   _____   _____

7. $\theta = 281°$

8. $\theta = -4°$

9. $\theta = 743°$

_____   _____   _____

Convert each measure from degrees to radians or from radians to degrees.

10. $\dfrac{5\pi}{12}$

11. 215°

12. $-\dfrac{29\pi}{18}$

_____   _____   _____

13. −180°

14. $\dfrac{5\pi}{3}$

15. $-\dfrac{7\pi}{6}$

_____   _____   _____

Solve.

16. San Antonio, Texas, is located about 30° north of the equator. If Earth's radius is about 3959 miles, approximately how many miles is San Antonio from the equator?

_____

LESSON 18-1

Angles of Rotation and Radian Measure

Practice and Problem Solving: C

Draw an angle with the given measure in standard position.

1. 550°   2. –645°   3. 715°

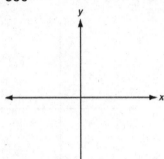   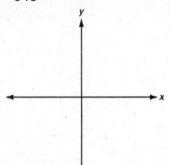   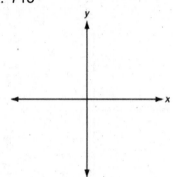

Find the measures of a positive angle and a negative angle that are coterminal with each given angle.

4. $\theta = 400°$ 5. $\theta = -360°$ 6. $\theta = -1010°$

_____   _____   _____

7. $\theta = 567°$ 8. $\theta = -164°$ 9. $\theta = 358°$

_____   _____   _____

Convert each measure from degrees to radians or from radians to degrees.

10. $-\dfrac{3\pi}{2}$ 11. 450°   12. $\dfrac{5\pi}{18}$

_____   _____   _____

13. –200°   14. $\dfrac{7\pi}{4}$ 15. $-\dfrac{11\pi}{6}$

_____   _____   _____

Solve.

16. A pendulum is 18 feet long. Its central angle is 44°. The pendulum makes one back and forth swing every 12 seconds. To the nearest foot, how far does the pendulum swing each minute?

_____

LESSON
18-2
Defining and Evaluating the Basic Trigonometric Functions
Practice and Problem Solving: A/B

Find the measure of the reference angle for each given angle.

1. $\theta = 220°$

2. $\theta = \dfrac{11\pi}{6}$

3. $\theta = -235°$

_____   _____   _____

4. $\theta = -\dfrac{2\pi}{3}$

5. $\theta = 590°$

6. $\theta = -\dfrac{13\pi}{4}$

_____   _____   _____

Find the exact value of each trigonometric function.

7. $\cos 120°$

8. $\sin \dfrac{4\pi}{3}$

9. $\sin 585°$

_____   _____   _____

10. $\tan 765°$

11. $\cos \dfrac{9\pi}{2}$

12. $\tan -\dfrac{5\pi}{6}$

_____   _____   _____

Use a calculator to evaluate each trigonometric function. Round to four decimal places.

13. $\sin 170°$

14. $\tan \dfrac{7\pi}{9}$

15. $\sin -\dfrac{8\pi}{3}$

_____   _____   _____

16. $\cos -71°$

17. $\tan 25°$

18. $\cos -\dfrac{21\pi}{5}$

_____   _____   _____

Solve. Assume each circle is centered at 0.

19. Find the exact coordinates of the point on a circle of radius 12.5 at an angle of 180°.

_____

20. Find the exact coordinates of the point on a circle of radius 7 at an angle of $\dfrac{5\pi}{4}$.

_____

LESSON 18-2 Defining and Evaluating the Basic Trigonometric Functions
Practice and Problem Solving: C

Find the measure of the reference angle for each given angle.

1. $\theta = 580°$

2. $\theta = -\dfrac{15\pi}{4}$

3. $\theta = -375°$

_____

_____

_____

4. $\theta = \dfrac{67\pi}{18}$

5. $\theta = -705°$

6. $\theta = -\dfrac{22\pi}{9}$

_____

_____

_____

Find the exact value of each trigonometric function.

7. $\cos 870°$

8. $\sin -\dfrac{19\pi}{6}$

9. $\sin -240°$

_____

_____

_____

10. $\tan -945°$

11. $\cos \dfrac{23\pi}{4}$

12. $\tan \dfrac{13\pi}{6}$

_____

_____

_____

Use a calculator to evaluate each trigonometric function. Round to four decimal places.

13. $\sin -840°$

14. $\tan \dfrac{19\pi}{18}$

15. $\sin \dfrac{341\pi}{60}$

_____

_____

_____

16. $\cos -760°$

17. $\tan -634°$

18. $\cos \dfrac{47\pi}{36}$

_____

_____

_____

Solve. Assume each circle is centered at 0.

19. Find the exact coordinates of the point on a circle of radius 7.25 at an angle of 315°.

_____

20. Find the exact coordinates of the point on a circle of radius 5 at an angle of $\dfrac{5\pi}{3}$.

_____

LESSON
18-3

Using a Pythagorean Identity

Practice and Problem Solving: A/B

Use the given value to calculate the values of the indicated trigonometric functions. Round your answers to three decimal places.

1. Given that $\cos \theta \approx 0.707$, where $0 < \theta < \dfrac{\pi}{2}$, find $\sin \theta$.

   _____

2. Given that $\sin \theta \approx -0.866$, where $\pi < \theta < \dfrac{3\pi}{2}$, find $\cos \theta$.

   _____

3. Given that $\tan \theta \approx 1.072$, where $0 < \theta < \dfrac{\pi}{2}$, find the values of $\sin \theta$ and $\cos \theta$.

   _____

4. Given that $\cos \theta \approx -0.485$, where $\dfrac{\pi}{2} < \theta < \pi$, find $\sin \theta$.

   _____

5. Given that $\tan \theta \approx -0.087$, where $\dfrac{3\pi}{2} < \theta < 2\pi$, find the values of $\sin \theta$ and $\cos \theta$.

   _____

6. Given that $\sin \theta = 0.5$, where $\dfrac{\pi}{2} < \theta < \pi$, find $\cos \theta$.

   _____

7. Given that $\sin \theta \approx -0.829$, where $\pi < \theta < \dfrac{3\pi}{2}$, find $\cos \theta$.

   _____

Solve.

8. The instant at which a waxed wood block on an inclined plane of wet snow begins to slide is represented by the equation $mg \sin \theta = \mu mg \cos \theta$, where θ represents the angle of the plane and μ is the coefficient of friction. What is $\cos \theta$ if $\mu = 0.52$ and $\sin \theta \approx 0.461$?

   _____

LESSON 18-3

Using a Pythagorean Identity

Practice and Problem Solving: C

Use the given value to calculate the values of the indicated trigonometric functions. Round your answers to three decimal places.

1. Given that $\sin \theta \approx 0.899$, where $0 < \theta < \dfrac{\pi}{2}$, find $\cos \theta$.

   _____

2. Given that $\cos \theta \approx -0.342$, where $\pi < \theta < \dfrac{3\pi}{2}$, find $\sin \theta$.

   _____

3. Given that $\tan \theta \approx 1.376$, where $0 < \theta < \dfrac{\pi}{2}$, find the values of $\sin \theta$ and $\cos \theta$.

   _____

4. Given that $\sin \theta \approx 0.839$, where $\dfrac{\pi}{2} < \theta < \pi$, find $\cos \theta$.

   _____

5. Given that $\tan \theta \approx -0.384$, where $\dfrac{3\pi}{2} < \theta < 2\pi$, find the values of $\sin \theta$ and $\cos \theta$.

   _____

6. Given that $\cos \theta \approx -0.438$, where $\dfrac{\pi}{2} < \theta < \pi$, find $\sin \theta$.

   _____

7. Given that $\cos \theta \approx -0.326$, where $\pi < \theta < \dfrac{3\pi}{2}$, find $\sin \theta$.

   _____

Solve.

8. Alan is using the equation $mg \sin \theta = \mu mg \cos \theta$ to determine the coefficient of friction, μ, between a flat rock and a metal ramp, where θ represents the angle of the ramp. Find μ to the nearest hundredth if $\sin \theta \approx 0.321$.

   _____

**LESSON
19-1**

Stretching, Compressing, and Reflecting Sine and Cosine Graphs
Practice and Problem Solving: A/B

Using $f(x) = \sin x$ or $g(x) = \cos x$ as a guide, graph each function.
Identify the amplitude and period.

1. $b(x) = -5\sin \pi x$

2. $k(x) = 3\cos 2\pi x$

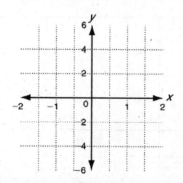

_____

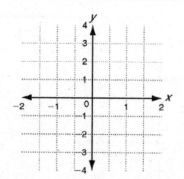

_____

Using $f(x) = \sin x$ or $g(x) = \cos x$ as a guide, graph each function.
Identify the period and asymptotes.

3. $k(x) = \sec \dfrac{x}{2}$

4. $q(x) = \dfrac{1}{2}\csc(2x)$

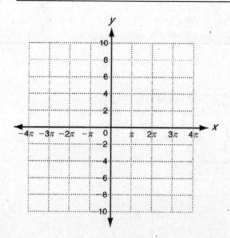

_____

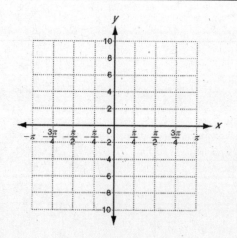

_____

Solve.

5. a. Use a sine function to graph a sound wave
   with a period of 0.002 second and an amplitude
   of 2 centimeters.

   b. Find the frequency in hertz for this sound wave.

   _____

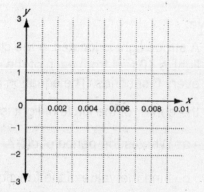

Name _____ Date _____ Class_____

19-1

Stretching, Compressing, and Reflecting Sine and Cosine Graphs

Practice and Problem Solving: C

Using $f(x) = \sin x$ or $f(x) = \cos x$ as a guide, graph each function.
Identify the amplitude, period, and x-intercepts.

1. $h(x) = \dfrac{1}{2}\cos(-\pi x)$

2. $q(x) = -\sin\left(\dfrac{\pi}{2}x\right)$

_____

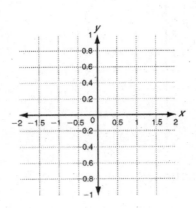

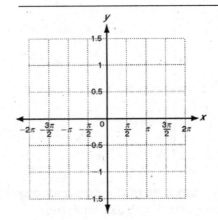

Using $f(x) = \cos x$ or $f(x) = \sin x$ as a guide, graph each function.
Identify the period and asymptotes.

3. $k(x) = \sec\dfrac{x}{4}$

4. $q(x) = 2\csc(2x)$

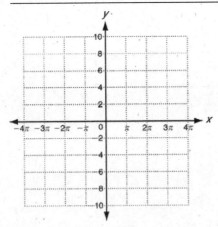

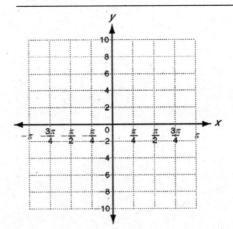

Solve.

5. A strobe light is located in the center of a square dance room. The rotating light is 40 feet from each of the 4 walls and completes one full rotation every 6 seconds. The equation representing the distance d in feet that the center of the circle of light is from the light source is $d(t) = 40\sec\left(\dfrac{\pi t}{3}\right)$.

   a. What is the period of $d(t)$? _____

   b. Find the value of the function at $t = 2.5$. _____

Original content Copyright © by Houghton Mifflin Harcourt. Additions and changes to the original content are the responsibility of the instructor.

118

LESSON 19-2

Stretching, Compressing, and Reflecting Tangent Graphs

Practice and Problem Solving: A/B

Write the function rule for the transformed tangent function shown.

Use the form $f(x) = a\tan\left(\dfrac{x}{b}\right)$.

1.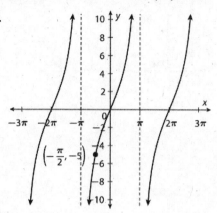

2.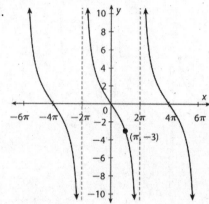

_____   _____

For each rule given for a transformed tangent function, find the asymptotes and reference points for one cycle. Then graph the function.

3. $f(x) = \dfrac{1}{2}\tan(3x)$

   Asymptotes: _____

   Reference Points: _____

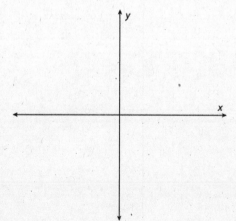

4. $f(x) = -4\tan\left(\dfrac{x}{5}\right)$

   Asymptotes: _____

   Reference Points: _____

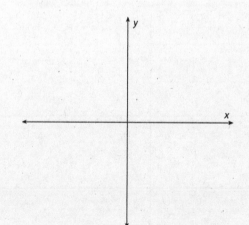

Name _____ Date _____ Class_____

Stretching, Compressing, and Reflecting Tangent Graphs

Practice and Problem Solving: C

Write the function rule for the transformed tangent function shown.

Use the form $f(x) = a\tan\left(\dfrac{x}{b}\right)$.

1.

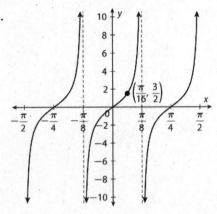

$\left(\dfrac{\pi}{16}, \dfrac{3}{2}\right)$

_____

2.

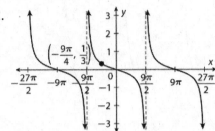

$\left(-\dfrac{9\pi}{4}, \dfrac{1}{3}\right)$

_____

For each rule given for a transformed tangent function, find the asymptotes and reference points for one cycle. Then graph the function.

3. $f(x) = -\dfrac{5}{4}\tan\left(\dfrac{x}{3}\right)$

Asymptotes: _____

Reference Points: _____

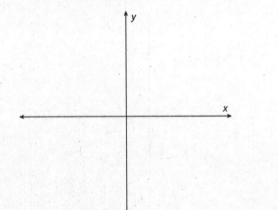

4. $f(x) = 2.2\tan(0.25x)$

Asymptotes: _____

Reference Points: _____

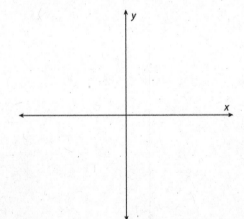

Name _____ Date _____ Class_____

LESSON 19-3 **Translating Trigonometric Graphs**
Practice and Problem Solving: A/B

For each rule given, identify the indicated points for one cycle. Then graph the function.

1. $f(x) = 2\sin\dfrac{1}{4}(x - 3\pi)$

   Starting point: _____

   Ending point: _____

   Middle point: _____

   Local minimum: _____

   Local maximum: _____

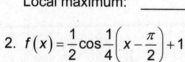

2. $f(x) = \dfrac{1}{2}\cos\dfrac{1}{4}\left(x - \dfrac{\pi}{2}\right) + 1$

   Starting point: _____

   Ending point: _____

   Middle point: _____

   1st Midline point: _____

   2nd midline point: _____

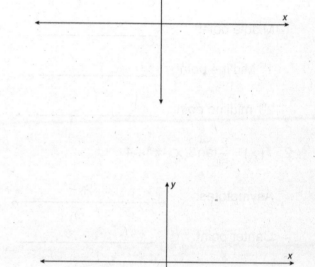

Write a function rule for the indicated trigonometric function.

3. Write a tangent function for the graph. (Hint: Use the key points and asymptotes shown on the graph.)

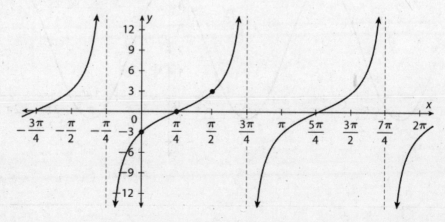

Translating Trigonometric Graphs

LESSON 19-3

Practice and Problem Solving: C

For each rule given, identify the indicated points or features for one cycle. Then graph the function.

1. $f(x) = \dfrac{3}{4}\cos 2\left(x + \dfrac{\pi}{3}\right) - 3$

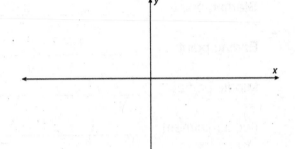

Starting point: _____

Ending point: _____

Middle point: _____

1st Midline point: _____

2nd midline point: _____

2. $f(x) = \dfrac{2}{5}\tan 3(x - \pi) + 4$

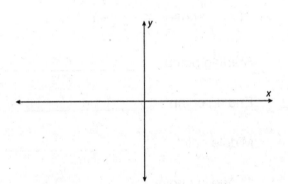

Asymptotes: _____

Center point: _____

Halfway point 1: _____

Halfway point 2: _____

Write a function rule for the indicated trigonometric function.

3. Write a sine function for the graph.

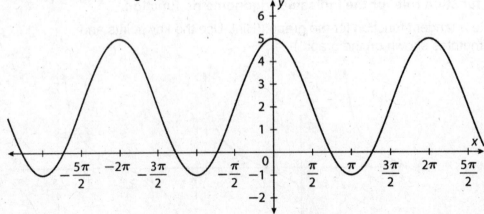

LESSON 19-4
Fitting Sine Functions to Data
Practice and Problem Solving: A/B

The data in the table represents the average daily temperatures T, in degrees Fahrenheit, for a city over a 12 month period. Use the data for Problems 1–5. Round to two decimal places when necessary.

Month	1	2	3	4	5	6	7	8	9	10	11	12
$T(°F)$	−7.8	−1.3	13.3	33	50.9	62.1	64.8	59.1	47.8	27.4	5	−4.2

1. Estimate the amplitude A, the period P, the phase shift h, and equation of the midline $k(x)$ for a sine function that models this data.

   _____

2. Use the factors to write a sine function that models the data.

   _____

3. Use the SinReg function on a graphing calculator to obtain a sine regression model for the data.

   _____

4. Rewrite the regression equation and compare it to the model you created using the factors.

   _____

5. Graph both models, along with the data points, on your graphing calculator. Sketch the result below.

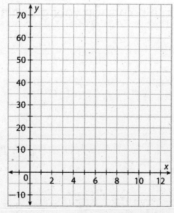

6. Use the intersect feature on your graphing calculator to find the intersection points of both models with the line $y = 10$. Compare and interpret the results.

   _____

   _____

Fitting Sine Functions to Data

Practice and Problem Solving: C

The data in the table represents the height, in meters, of a pendulum as it swings over time, in seconds. Use the data for Problems 1–6. Round to three decimal places when necessary.

Time (sec)	0.12	0.24	0.36	0.42	0.48	0.6	0.72
Height (m)	0.663	1.167	0.995	0.864	0.655	1.215	0.929

	0.84	0.96	1.08	1.14	1.2	1.32	1.44
	0.659	1.254	0.865	0.755	0.676	1.281	0.807

1. Estimate the amplitude A, the period P, the phase shift h, and equation of the midline $k(x)$ for a sine function that models this data.

_____

2. Use the factors to write a sine function that models the data.

_____

3. Use the SinReg function on a graphing calculator to obtain a sine regression model for the data.

_____

4. Rewrite the regression equation and compare it to the model you created using the factors.

_____

5. Graph both models, along with the data points, on your graphing calculator. Sketch the result below.

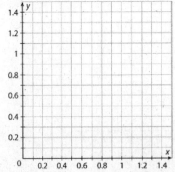

6. For each model, find the first two times the pendulum reaches a height of 1.2 meters. Compare your result to the graphs of the models. How do you think the results would differ as time increases?

_____

_____

Data-Gathering Techniques

Practice and Problem Solving: A/B

A school committee is planning an academic Olympics to raise money for the school. The committee surveys a random sample of 40 classrooms in which the students would need to participate as a team. The survey results show how many students in each class would be interested in participating and, if so, what subject the team prefers (math, history, or computer science) and how many of the three subjects the teams would participate in. Of the 24 classrooms surveyed, 6 indicated an interest in participating. The table lists the data for those 6 classrooms.

Preferred Subject	Number of Students Interested in Participating	Number of Academic Subjects Students Would Participate In
Math	6	1
Computer science	4	2
Math	5	1
History	9	3
History	2	2
Computer science	3	2

1. Calculate the proportion of classrooms that indicated an interest in participating. Round to the nearest thousandth.

   _____

2. Calculate the proportion of those interested in participating who prefer history. Round to the nearest thousandth.

   _____

3. If 1500 students are in the school, predict the number of students who would participate that prefer history.

   _____

4. For those with an interest in participating, calculate the mean number of classroom members who might participate and the mean number of academic subjects that those classroom members might participate in. Round to the nearest tenth.

   _____

5. If the committee receives $15 vouchers for each student who participates, predict the amount that will be raised from the events.

   _____

Data-Gathering Techniques

LESSON 20-1

Practice and Problem Solving: C

A hotel chain is planning a promotional event to raise its customer base. The chain surveys a random sample of 4500 households from a community to see if adults would travel for a nominal fee in exchange for attending a promotional seminar. The survey results show how many adults in each household would be interested in participating and, if so, what location is preferred (ocean, mountains, and city) and how many of the three locations the participants would go to. Of the 27 households surveyed, 7 indicated an interest in participating. The table lists the data for those 7 households.

Preferred Location	Number of Adults Interested in Participating	Number of Locations Participants Would Go To
Ocean	2	1
Mountains	4	3
City	3	2
Mountains	1	1
City	3	1
Ocean	4	2
Ocean	2	3

1. Calculate the proportion of households that indicated an interest in participating. Round to the nearest thousandth.

   _____

2. Calculate the proportion of those interested in participating who prefer traveling to the ocean. Round to the nearest thousandth.

   _____

3. If approximately 11,250 adults live in the community, predict the number who would participate that prefer traveling to the ocean.

   _____

4. For those with an interest in participating, calculate the mean number of household members who might participate and the mean number of locations that those household members might go to. Round to the nearest tenth.

   _____

5. If the nominal fee for travel is $50 for each adult that participates, predict the amount that the hotel chain can expect from the promotion.

   _____

Shape, Center, and Spread
LESSON 20-2
Practice and Problem Solving: A/B

Solve each problem. Round answers to two decimal places.

1. The table below shows a major league baseball player's season home run totals for the first 14 years of his career.

Season	1	2	3	4	5	6	7	8	9	10	11	12	13	14
Home Runs	18	22	21	28	30	29	32	40	33	34	28	29	22	20

a. Find the mean, median, standard deviation, and interquartile range for the data.

_____

b. Make a line plot for the data.

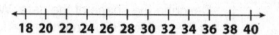

18 20 22 24 26 28 30 32 34 36 38 40

2. For three weeks, the number of calls per day to a fire and rescue service were recorded. The results are shown below.

Calls for Service										
5	17	2	12	0	6	3	8	15	1	4
19	16	8	2	11	13	18	3	10	6	

a. Find the mean, median, standard deviation, and interquartile range for the data.

b. Draw a histogram for the data. Is the distribution symmetrical? Explain.

_____

_____

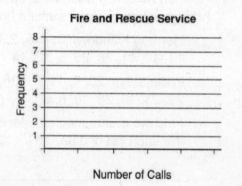

Fire and Rescue Service

Number of Calls

3. For 10 weeks, Kay recorded the amount of gas, in gallons, she used while driving. The results were 10, 14, 18, 12, 20, 24, 9, 25, 14, 16.

a. Find the mean, median, standard deviation, and interquartile range for the data.

_____

b. Make a box plot for the data. What type of shape does the box plot show? Explain.

_____

_____

Shape, Center, and Spread

Practice and Problem Solving: C

Solve each problem. Round answers to two decimal places.

1. The line plot below shows the ages of 20 presidents of the United
   States upon first taking office.

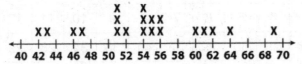

   a. Find the mean, median, standard deviation, and interquartile range for
       the data.

   _____

   b. Describe the shape of the data. What does the shape tell you in terms
       of the problem situation?

   _____

   c. A president not included in the data set above is Grover Cleveland,
       who took office on March 4, 1893. Based on your work so far, make an
       educated guess as to his age that day. Explain your reasoning. Then
       find his age on the Internet.

   _____

2. Harmon Killebrew and Willie Mays were two of baseball's greatest
   home run hitters. Their season home run totals are shown below.

   Harmon Killebrew: 0, 4, 5, 2, 0, 42, 31, 46, 48, 45, 49, 25, 39, 44,
   17, 49, 41, 28, 26, 5, 13, 14

   Willie Mays: 20, 4, 41, 51, 36, 35, 29, 34, 29, 40, 49, 38, 47, 52, 37,
   22, 23, 13, 28, 18, 8, 6

   a. Find the mean, median, standard deviation, and interquartile range for
       the each set of data.

   _____

   b. Make a double box plot for Killebrew and Mays.

   ⟵————————————————⟶

   c. Use the box plots to describe how Killebrew and Mays were alike and
       different in their home run production.

   _____

Probability Distributions

Practice and Problem Solving: A/B

A spinner has three equal sections, labeled 1, 2, and 3. You spin the spinner twice and find the absolute value of the difference of the two numbers the spinner lands on. Use this information for Problems 1–4.

1. Let X be a random variable that represents the absolute value of the difference of the two numbers. What are the possible values of X?

   _____

2. Fill in the table for the probability distribution.

Absolute Value of the Difference			
Probability			

3. Make a histogram of the probability distribution.

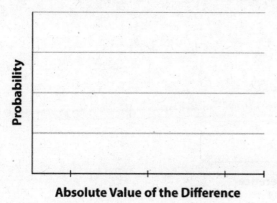

   Absolute Value of the Difference

4. What is the probability that the absolute value of the difference is not 2? How is this probability represented in the histogram?

   _____

Solve.

5. Sports drinks are purchased by 3 out of 4 students using the campus snack machines. There are 3 students at the machines now. Use the formula for binomial probability, $P(r) = {}_nC_r p^r q^{n-r}$, to determine the probability that at least 2 of the students will buy a sports drink.

   _____

Probability Distributions

Practice and Problem Solving: C

A spinner has four equal sections, labeled 1, 2, 3, and 4. You spin the spinner twice and find the absolute value of the difference of the two numbers the spinner lands on. Use this information for Problems 1–4.

1. Let X be a random variable that represents the absolute value of the difference of the two numbers. What are the possible values of X?

   _____

2. Fill in the table for the probability distribution.

Absolute Value of the Difference				
Probability				

3. Make a histogram of the probability distribution.

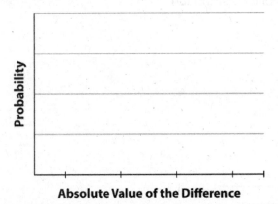

Absolute Value of the Difference

4. What is the probability that the absolute value of the difference is not 1? How is this probability represented in the histogram?

   _____

Solve.

5. Sales records for the snack machines show that 1 out of every 6 students buys a bag of trail mix. There are 5 students waiting to use the machines.

   a. What is the probability of exactly 3 students buying a bag of trail mix?

   _____

   b. What is the probability of at least 1 student buying a bag of trail mix?

   _____

Name _____ Date _____ Class_____

Normal Distributions
Practice and Problem Solving: A/B

At a shoe factory, the number of various shoe sizes produced is normally distributed with a mean of size 9 and a standard deviation of 1.5 sizes. Use this information for Problems 1–3.

1. What is the probability that a shoe size will be larger than size 10.5 if a supervisor chooses a shoe at random?

   _____

2. What is the probability that a shoe size will be smaller than size 6 if a supervisor chooses a shoe at random?

   _____

3. What is the probability that a shoe size will be between sizes 7.5 and 12 if a supervisor chooses a shoe at random?

   _____

Scores on a test are normally distributed with a mean of 78 and a standard deviation of 8. Use the table below to find each probability.

z	−2.5	−2	−1.5	−1	−0.5	0	0.5	1	1.5	2	2.5
Area	0.01	0.02	0.07	0.16	0.31	0.5	0.69	0.84	0.93	0.98	0.99

4. A randomly selected student scored below 90. _____

5. A randomly selected student scored above 86. _____

6. A randomly selected student scored between 86 and 90. _____

7. A randomly selected student scored between 74 and 78. _____

Solve.

8. The ages of 20 people who sing in the choir are given below. If the mean of all the ages of the people in the choir is 40 years and the standard deviation is 12 years, do the data appear to be normally distributed? Explain.

25	37	32	38	51
62	52	54	29	35
39	58	30	28	34
34	36	37	64	25

Name _____ Date _____ Class_____

Normal Distributions

Practice and Problem Solving: C

The stride lengths, in feet, in a group of adult males are normally distributed with a mean of 2.5 feet and a standard deviation of 0.04 feet. Use this information for Problems 1–3.

1. What is the probability that the stride length of a randomly selected adult male is less than 2.58 feet?

   _____

2. What is the probability that the stride length of a randomly selected adult male is between 2.38 feet and 2.46 feet?

   _____

3. What is the probability that the stride length of a randomly selected adult male is between 2.42 feet and 2.54 feet?

   _____

Scores on a test are normally distributed with a mean of 81.2 and a standard deviation of 3.6. Use the table below to find each probability.

z	−2.5	−2	−1.5	−1	−0.5	0	0.5	1	1.5	2	2.5
Area	0.01	0.02	0.07	0.16	0.31	0.5	0.69	0.84	0.93	0.98	0.99

4. A randomly selected student scored below 74.   _____

5. A randomly selected student scored above 88.4.   _____

6. A randomly selected student scored between 81.2 and 84.8.   _____

7. A randomly selected student scored between 77.6 and 88.4.   _____

Solve.

8. The stride lengths, in feet, in a group of adult females are given below. If standard deviation in the stride lengths is 0.02 ft, do the data appear to be normally distributed? Explain.

1.78	1.85	1.87	1.96	2.02
2.04	2.05	2.05	2.17	2.19
2.23	2.25	2.26	2.28	2.35
2.38	2.41	2.43	2.55	2.68

Sampling Distributions
Practice and Problem Solving: A/B

**A study showed that the mean age of visitors at a large art museum is
42 years old with a standard deviation of 6.2 years. You choose a
random sample of 25 visitors. Use this information for Problems 1–4.**

1. Find the mean of the sampling distribution of the sample mean.

   _____

2. Find the standard error of the mean.

   _____

3. What interval captures 95% of the means for random samples of
   25 visitors?

   _____

4. What is the probability that your sample has a mean age of at most
   45 years?

   _____

**About 38% of students at a large school play an instrument. Chelsea
chooses a random sample of 70 students at the school. Use this
information for Problems 5–9.**

5. Find the mean of the sampling distribution of the sample proportion.

   _____

6. Find the standard error of the proportion.

   _____

7. What is the probability that Chelsea's sample has more than
   25 students who play an instrument?

   _____

8. What is the probability that Chelsea's sample has a proportion
   between 25% and 35%?

   _____

9. Find the interval that captures 68% of the proportions for random
   samples of 70 students.

   _____

LESSON 21-3

Sampling Distributions

Practice and Problem Solving: C

The meanlength of songs played by a radio station is 3.7 minutes with a standard deviation of 1.3 minutes. The station chooses a random sample of 30 songs. Use this information for Problems 1–5.

1. Find the mean of the sampling distribution of the sample mean.

   _____

2. Find the standard error of the mean.

   _____

3. What interval captures 99.7% of the means for random samples of 30 songs?

   _____

4. What is the probability that the sample has a mean songlength between 3 and 3.5 minutes?

   _____

5. What is the probability that the total airtime of the 30 randomly selected songs exceeds 126 minutes?

   _____

About 23 out of every 100 students at Rafael's high school have a blog. Rafael chooses a random sample of 85 students at his high school. Use this information for Problems 6–9.

6. Find the mean of the sampling distribution of the sample proportion.

   _____

7. Find the standard error of the proportion.

   _____

8. What is the probability that Rafael's sample has at most 17 students who have a blog?

   _____

9. What is the probability that Rafael's sample has between 20 and 30 students who have a blog?

   _____

Confidence Intervals and Margins of Error

Practice and Problem Solving: A/B

Find the confidence interval for the proportion or the mean in each situation. Round to two decimal places.

1. Rachael surveys a random sample of 80 students at her high school and finds that 18 of the students have a part-time job. Find a 90% confidence interval for the proportion p of students at Rachael's school who have a part-time job.

_____

2. A quality control team of a light bulb manufacturer measures the life of 125 randomly selected incandescent bulbs and finds that the mean amount of bulb life is 1600 hours. Given that the population standard deviation is 200 hours, find a 99% confidence interval for the mean amount of incandescent bulb life.

_____

Find the appropriate sample size for each situation. Round to the nearest whole number.

3. The marketing department of an internet radio station wants to know the percent of residents in a large state who listen to internet radio. Based on data from other states, they estimate $\hat{p} = 0.62$. They are aiming for a 95% confidence interval and a margin of error of 4%. How many state residents should they survey?

_____

4. Henry owns a sport supply store and wants to know the mean amount of revenue per week. He is aiming for a 90% confidence interval and a margin of error of $200. Given that the population standard deviation is $600, what sample size should Henry use?

_____

Solve. Round to three decimal places.

5. A group of researchers from a major health organization surveys a random sample of 435 adult residents of a state to find the percent of people who get a check-up at least once a year. Suppose the proportion p of the population who get a check-up at least once a year is 28.3%. What are the reasonably likely values of $\hat{p}$ that fall within 2 standard deviations of p?

_____

LESSON 22-1

Confidence Intervals and Margins of Error

Practice and Problem Solving: C

Find the confidence interval for the proportion or the mean in each situation. Round to two decimal places.

1. In a random sample of 1625 families from a large state, approximately 273 of the families travel at least 300 miles away from home once or more each year. Find a 95% confidence interval for the proportion p of families in the state that travel at least 300 miles away from home once or more each year.

   _____

2. Garrett surveys 184 randomly selected residents in his city and finds that the mean amount of time spent watching television per week is 14 hours, 45 minutes. Given that the population standard deviation is 42 minutes, find a 90% confidence interval for the mean amount of hours residents of Garrett's city spend watching television per week.

   _____

Find the appropriate sample size for each situation. Round to the nearest whole number.

3. A researcher wants to know the percent of adults with bank accounts in the United States that do all or most of their banking online. Based on a similar recent study, he estimates $\hat{p} = 0.25$. He is aiming for a 99% confidence interval and a margin of error of 2.25%. How many adults with bank accounts should the researcher survey?

   _____

4. Charlene manages the marketing division of a tent manufacturing company and wants to know the mean number of minutes it takes customers to assemble a two-man tent. She is aiming for a 95% confidence interval and a margin of error of 0.25 minutes. Through past experience, Charlene knows that the population standard deviation is 1.3 minutes. What sample size should Charlene use?

   _____

Solve. Round to three decimal places.

5. A research group surveys a random sample of 675 teenagers in a state to find the percent of teens that eat vegetables less than once daily. Suppose the proportion p of the population who eat vegetables less than once daily is 33.2%. What are the reasonably likely values of $\hat{p}$ that fall within 2 standard deviations of p?

   _____

LESSON 22-2

Surveys, Experiments, and Observational Studies

Practice and Problem Solving: A/B

Explain whether each situation is an experiment or an observational study.

1. A teacher asks her students to write down everything they eat in a day and then calculate the total number of calories consumed.

   _____

2. A marine biologist visits a certain beach in Florida every year and counts the number of eggs in sea turtle nests.

   _____

3. The cafeteria manager of a high school wants to find out if high prices are keeping students from using the cafeteria. Fifty students are chosen at random to receive half-price lunch passes every day for a month. The manager then records the number of passes used.

   _____

The studies described below are randomized comparative experiments. Describe the treatment, the characteristic of interest, the treatment group, and the control group.

4. A medical researcher collects data about a certain medicine. She asks 10 patients to take the medicine and another 10 patients to take a placebo (a sugar pill known to have no effect). None of the patients knows which group he or she is in. At the end of six months, the group taking the medicine showed more improvement in its symptoms than the group taking the placebo.

   _____

5. A department store wants to increase its sales. It assembled 100 of its best credit card customers and randomly divided them into two groups of 50. One group was allowed to use a special website for ordering goods and paying bills and the other group was not. At the end of six months, the group using the special website made 40% more purchases than the other group.

   _____

Explain whether the research topic is best addressed through an experiment or an observational study. Then explain how you would set up the experiment or observational study.

6. Does getting less than 7 hours of sleep per night affect how students perform in their morning classes?

   _____

   _____

7. Do people who take zinc as a dietary supplement each day have fewer colds than people who do not take zinc supplements?

   _____

   _____

Surveys, Experiments, and Observational Studies
Practice and Problem Solving: C

Explain whether each situation is an experiment or an observational study.

1. A school guidance counselor wants to know whether students with older siblings who went away to college are more likely to want to go away to college themselves. She interviews students about whether they have older siblings who went away to college and whether they are planning to themselves.

   _____

2. The manager of a grocery store wants to know if a product's location in the store affects how well the product sells. He first tracks how many of a certain item sells over a month when the display is located where it always has been. He then moves the display to the front of the store so that customers see it when they first enter. He again tracks how many of the items sell over a month and compares the numbers.

   _____

3. A researcher wants to know whether teens in warmer climates tend to be more physically active than teens in colder climates. She randomly selects 100 teens in states with typically colder climates and 100 teens in 3 states with typically warmer climates and surveys them all about their levels of activity.

   _____

The studies described below are randomized comparative experiments. Describe the treatment, the characteristic of interest, the treatment group, and the control group.

4. A researcher wants to know whether background noise affects people's abilities to complete simple cognitive tasks. She has 20 people perform a series of tasks. Ten randomly selected subjects perform the tasks in a quiet room. The other 10 perform the tasks in a room that has traffic noise outside and muffled voices coming from the room next door. She records how successful each group of subjects is in completing the assigned tasks.

   _____

5. The members of a transportation department in a city are deciding whether it will save them money in the long run to use a new, more expensive asphalt mixture to pave their roads. Of 6 city roads scheduled for repaving, they pave 3 with the new asphalt and 3 with the old asphalt. After one year's wear, they study the conditions of the roads.

   _____

Explain whether the research topic is best addressed through an experiment or an observational study. Then explain how you would set up the experiment or observational study.

6. Will offering access to internet-equipped computers to non-members of a library increase the number of new members?

   _____

   _____

   _____

Determining the Significance of Experimental Results

LESSON 22-3

Practice and Problem Solving: A/B

Mr. Kaplan is supervising an experiment in his science class in order to find out whether adding salt to water causes the water to boil more quickly. Each student in the class records how long it takes his or her beaker of water to boil when placed on a burner. Half of the students do not add salt to the water and half of the students add a teaspoon of salt to the water. The results of the experiment, in seconds, are shown below. Use this information for Problems 1–2.

Control	65	78	62	71	73
Treatment	63	70	74	68	69

1. State the null hypothesis for the experiment.

   _____

2. Calculate the mean of the control group, $\overline{x}_C$, and the treatment group, $\overline{x}_T$. Does the result of the experiment appear to be statistically significant?

   _____

A research team is testing whether a fuel additive has a significant effect on a car's gas mileage. The gas mileage, in miles per gallon (mpg), of a certain make and model of car is known to have a mean mileage of 22.4 mpg. A random sample of that model car was given the treatment. The result was a mean mileage of 26.7 mpg. Use this information for Problems 3–6.

3. State the null hypothesis for the experiment.

   _____

4. State the mean mileage for the treatment group, $\overline{x}_T$, and the mean mileage for the control group, $\overline{x}_C$. Then find the difference of the means.

   _____

5. Given that the null hypothesis is true, the sampling distribution for the difference of mileage is normal with a mean of 0 and a standard error of 1.9. What interval captures 95% of the differences of means in the sampling distribution?

   _____

6. Determine whether the result is statistically significant, and state a conclusion about whether the null hypothesis should be rejected.

   _____

Determining the Significance of Experimental Results

LESSON 22-3

Practice and Problem Solving: C

A school is testing whether a new curriculum is successful in raising final exam scores. The data show the scores of the classes that were taught with the new curriculum and the classes that continued to use the old curriculum. Use this information for Problems 1–2.

Control	72	85	72	73	90	64	75	81	70
Treatment	97	88	82	90	79	83	99	82	86

1. State the null hypothesis for the experiment.

   _____

2. Calculate the mean of the control group $\bar{x}_C$ and the treatment group $\bar{x}_T$.
   Does the result of the experiment appear to be statistically significant?

   _____

GoBo Toy Company manufactures rubber balls. GoBo claims its new rubber will cause its balls to bounce significantly higher than the balls made of its old rubber. In an experiment, bounce heights were measured from random samples of balls made of the old rubber and the new rubber. The balls made of the old rubber had a mean bounce height of 137.16 centimeters. The balls made of the new rubber had a mean bounce height of 149.35 centimeters. Use this information for Problems 3–6.

3. State the null hypothesis for the experiment.

   _____

4. State the mean bounce height for the treatment group $\bar{x}_T$ and the mean bounce height for the control group $\bar{x}_C$. Then find the difference of the means.

   _____

5. Given that the null hypothesis is true, the resampling distribution for the difference in bounce heights is normal with a mean of 0 and a standard error of 5.78. What interval captures 95% of the differences of means in the resampling distribution?

   _____

6. Determine whether the result is statistically significant, and state a conclusion about whether the null hypothesis should be rejected.

   _____

Using Probability to Make Fair Decisions

Practice and Problem Solving: A/B

Determine whether the method of distributing tickets is fair or not fair.

1. Tickets for female customers only   _____

2. Three tickets for each customer   _____

3. Tickets for every other customer   _____

There are five members in a math club. Determine which methods are fair for choosing one of the members randomly to be the team captain.

4. Assign four of the members one number each and assign
   one member two numbers.   _____

5. Assign each member a number on a strip of paper. Choose one of the
   strips of paper at random from a bowl.   _____

6. Choose the member who is the oldest.   _____

Four friends want to go out to dinner. They each want to go to a different restaurant. Which methods are fair for choosing which restaurant to go to?

7. Choose the closest restaurant.

_____

8. Use a spinner with four equal pie slices, each representing a different
   restaurant.

_____

9. Use a spinner with three equal pie slices, representing the top three
   restaurants.

_____

10. Write each restaurant name on its own slip of paper and draw a slip of
    paper at random.

_____

Using Probability to Make Fair Decisions
Practice and Problem Solving: C

There are 250 customers who can participate in a prize drawing. Determine whether the method of distributing tickets is fair or not fair.

1. Four tickets for every customer until 100 customers have been given tickets. _____

2. Two tickets are given to each of the first 150 customers. Then 2 tickets each for the remaining customers. _____

3. One ticket for customers whose last name starts with A–K. One ticket for customers whose last name starts with L–Z. _____

Two boys and four girls are on a quiz bowl team. Determine which methods are fair for choosing one of the members randomly to be the team captain.

4. Flip a coin to determine whether the captain will be a boy or girl and write the names of the winning gender on slips of paper. Then choose the captain by drawing a name from a box. _____

5. Since there are more girls, assign each girl a number and choose that number at random from a box. _____

6. Assign each member a different number from 1–6. Roll a die to determine the winner. _____

7. Give each boy two tickets and each girl one ticket. Draw a ticket at random from a box. _____

A committee planning a spring dance has three male students, five female students, and two teachers on it. The committee leader will be chosen at random and must be a student. Which methods are fair for choosing the committee leader?

8. A spinner with ten equal-size pie slices, one for each committee member.

_____

9. Assigning each male student a number between 1 and 3, assigning a female student a number between 7 and 11, and drawing one of these numbers at random from a box.

_____

10. Assigning each male student two numbers and each female student one number, and drawing one of these numbers at random from a box.

_____

Analyzing Decisions

Practice and Problem Solving: A/B

A restaurant has a beverage machine that works well 90% of the time. The owners bought a new beverage machine that works well 94% of the time. Each machine is used 50% of the time.

For Problems 1–4, use Bayes' Theorem to find each probability. Round your answer to the nearest tenth of a percent.

1. Old machine malfunctioned   _____

2. New machine malfunctioned   _____

3. Old machine worked well   _____

4. New machine worked well   _____

A small apartment building has two washing machines. Washing Machine A malfunctions 13% of the time. Washing Machine B malfunctions 18% of the time. Washing Machine A is used 60% of the time. Washing Machine B is used 40% of the time.

For problems 5–8, use Bayes' Theorem to find each probability. Round your answer to the nearest tenth of a percent.

5. Machine A malfunctioned.   _____

6. Machine B malfunctioned.   _____

7. Machine A worked well.   _____

8. Machine B worked well.   _____

A prize machine at a festival has a probability of 34% of awarding a customer a ticket for a free meal. An older prize machine has a probability of 45% of awarding a customer a ticket for a free meal. Each machine is used 50% of the time.

9. The next prize drawn is a ticket for a free meal. Use Bayes' Theorem
   to determine the probability that the new machine awarded this ticket.

   _____

Analyzing Decisions

LESSON 23-2

Practice and Problem Solving: C

A bank has a coin counting machine that works well 95% of the time. They have an older coin counting machine that malfunctions 9% of the time. The new machine is used 75% of the time and the old machine is used the remaining percentage of time.

For Problems 1–4, use Bayes' Theorem to find each probability. Round your answer to the nearest tenth of a percent.

1. New machine worked well   _____

2. Old machine malfunctioned   _____

3. New machine malfunction   _____

4. Old machine worked well   _____

Use the following situation for Problems 5–7.

A movie theatre has two popcorn machines. Popcorn Machine A works well 96% of the time. Popcorn Machine B works well 92% of the time. Popcorn Machine A is used 80% of the time. The movie theater owner complains that the popcorn produced has too many kernels that did not pop.

5. Find the probability that Popcorn Machine A was used to make the popcorn   _____

6. Find the probability that Popcorn Machine B was used to make the popcorn   _____

7. The owner blamed Popcorn Machine A for the kernels that did not pop. Was the owner correct in doing so? Explain your answer.   _____

A prize machine at a festival has a probability of 70% of awarding a customer a ticket for a free meal. A new prize machine has a probability of 40% of awarding a customer a ticket for something other than a free meal. The new prize machine is used 80% of the time. Round your answer to the nearest percent.

8. The next prize drawn is a ticket for a free meal. Use Bayes' Theorem to determine the probability that the new machine awarded this ticket.

_____

LESSON 24-1

Central Angles and Inscribed Angles

Practice and Problem Solving: A/B

Refer to the figure for Problems 1–3. C is the center of the circle.

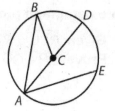

1. Name the chord(s). _____

2. Name the central angle(s). _____

3. Name the inscribed angle(s). _____

For each figure, determine the indicated measures.

4.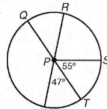

$m\overset{\frown}{QS} = $ _____

$m\overset{\frown}{RQT} = $ _____

5.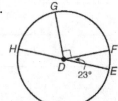

$m\overset{\frown}{HG} = $ _____

$m\overset{\frown}{FEH} = $ _____

6.

$m\angle CED = $ _____

$m\overset{\frown}{DEA} = $ _____

7.

$m\angle FGI = $ _____

$m\overset{\frown}{GH} = $ _____

Find the unknown value.

8.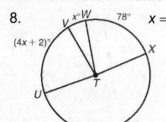

$x = $ _____

9.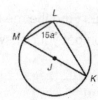

$a = $ _____

The figure shows a passenger airplane's flight path on a circular radar screen in an air traffic control tower.

10. What is $m\overset{\frown}{MJ}$? _____

11. What is $m\angle LJK$? _____

12. What is $m\angle LNK$? _____

LESSON
24-1

Central Angles and Inscribed Angles

Practice and Problem Solving: C

Write paragraph proofs for Problems 1 and 2.

1. **Given:** $\overarc{RSU} \cong \overarc{RTU}$
   Prove: $\odot P \cong \odot Q$

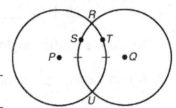

_____

_____

_____

_____

_____

2. **Given:** $\overline{AC} \cong \overline{AD}$
   Prove: $\angle ABC \cong \angle AED$

_____

_____

_____

_____

_____

3. In $\odot C$, $\triangle ABE \sim \triangle CDE$. Find the measures for $\angle BAE$, $\angle EBA$, and $\angle BEA$. Explain how you got your answers.

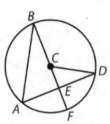

_____

_____

_____

_____

LESSON
24-2

Angles in Inscribed Quadrilaterals
Practice and Problem Solving: A/B

Each quadrilateral described is inscribed in a circle. Determine the angle measures.

1. Quadrilateral *ABCD* has m∠*A* = 53° and m∠*B* = 82°.

   m∠*C* = _____   m∠*D* = _____

2. Quadrilateral *RSTU* has m∠*S* = 104° and m∠*T* = 55°.

   m∠*R* = _____   m∠*U* = _____

3. Quadrilateral *JKLM* has m∠*J* = 90° and ∠*K* ≅ ∠*M*.

   m∠*K* = _____   m∠*L* = _____   m∠*M* = _____

**Determine whether each quadrilateral can be inscribed in a circle.
If it cannot be determined, say so.**

4. 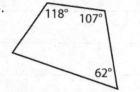 _____

5. 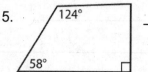 _____

6. 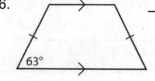 _____

7.   _____

For each inscribed quadrilateral, determine the angle measures.

8.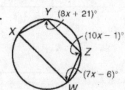

   m∠*X* = _____

   m∠*Y* = _____

   m∠*Z* = _____

   m∠*W* = _____

9.

   m∠*C* = _____

   m∠*D* = _____

   m∠*E* = _____

   m∠*F* = _____

10.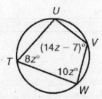

    m∠*T* = _____

    m∠*U* = _____

    m∠*V* = _____

    m∠*W* = _____

11.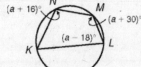

    m∠*K* = _____

    m∠*L* = _____

    m∠*M* = _____

    m∠*N* = _____

Name _____ Date _____ Class_____

24-2

Angles in Inscribed Quadrilaterals

Practice and Problem Solving: C

For each inscribed quadrilateral, find the measure of its angles.

1.

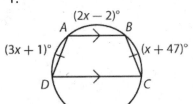

m∠A = _____   2.   m∠R = _____

m∠B = _____   m∠S = _____

m∠C = _____   m∠T = _____

m∠D = _____   m∠U = _____

For each quadrilateral described, tell whether it can be inscribed in a circle. If so, describe a method for doing so using a compass and straightedge. Then draw an example.

3. a parallelogram that is not a rectangle or a square

_____

_____

_____

_____

4. a kite

_____

_____

_____

_____

5. a trapezoid

_____

_____

_____

_____

Original content Copyright © by Houghton Mifflin Harcourt. Additions and changes to the original content are the responsibility of the instructor.

**LESSON
24-3**
Tangents and Circumscribed Angles
Practice and Problem Solving: A/B

Refer to the figure for Problems 1–4. $\overline{AB}$ is tangent to ⊙*C*
at point *B* and $\overline{AD}$ is tangent to ⊙*C* at point *B*. Determine
the angle measures.

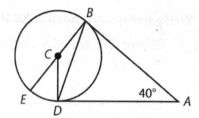

1. m∠*ABC* = _____

2. m∠*DCB* = _____

3. m∠*BDA* = _____

4. m∠*CDB* = _____

Refer to the figure for Problems 5–8. $\overline{AB}$ is tangent to
⊙*C* at point *B* and $\overline{AD}$ is tangent to ⊙*C* at point *B*.
Determine the angle measures.

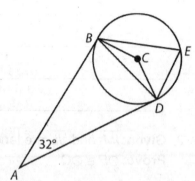

5. m∠*BCD* = _____

6. m∠*CDA* = _____

7. m∠*BED* = _____

8. m∠*DBA* = _____

In Problems 9 and 10, $\overline{QM}$ is tangent to ⊙*P* at point *M* and $\overline{QN}$ is
tangent to ⊙*P* at point *P*. Solve for the variable and determine the
angle measures.

9.

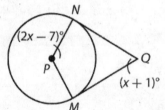

x = _____   m∠*NQM* = _____

m∠*PNQ* = _____   m∠*NPM* = _____

10.

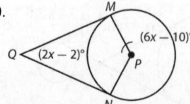

x = _____   m∠*MQN* = _____

m∠*QMP* = _____   m∠*NPM* = _____

In Problems 11 and 12, $\overline{EF}$ is tangent to ⊙*H* at point *F* and $\overline{EG}$ is
tangent to ⊙*H* at point *G*. Determine the length of $\overline{EF}$.

11.

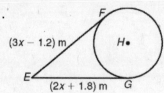

EF = _____

12.

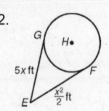

EF = _____

LESSON 24-3

Tangents and Circumscribed Angles
Practice and Problem Solving: C

Write paragraph proofs for Problems 1 and 2.

1. **Given:** $\overline{QR}$ and $\overline{QS}$ are tangent to $\odot P$; $\angle PQR \cong \angle TUS$.
   Prove: $m\angle RQS = 60°$

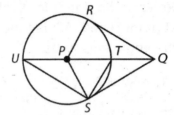

_____

_____

_____

_____

_____

2. **Given:** $\overline{IM}$ and $\overline{JL}$ are tangent to $\odot G$ and $\odot H$.
   Prove: $\odot P \cong \odot Q$

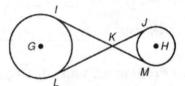

_____

_____

_____

_____

_____

In Problems 3 and 4, assume that the segments appearing to be tangent are tangent. Determine the length.

3.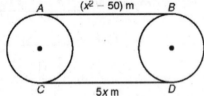

4.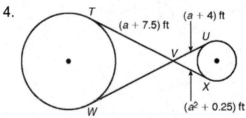

$CD =$ _____ $UW =$ _____

LESSON 24-4

Segment Relationships in Circles

Practice and Problem Solving: A/B

For each figure, determine the value of the variable and the indicated lengths by applying the Chord-Chord Product Theorem.

1.

$x =$ _____

$AD =$ _____

$BE =$ _____

2.

$y =$ _____

$FH =$ _____

$GI =$ _____

3.

$z =$ _____

$PS =$ _____

$RT =$ _____

4.

$m =$ _____

$UW =$ _____

$VX =$ _____

For each figure, determine the value of the variable and the indicated lengths by applying the Secant-Secant Product Theorem.

5.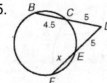

$x =$ _____

$BD =$ _____

$FD =$ _____

6.

$y =$ _____

$GJ =$ _____

$GK =$ _____

7.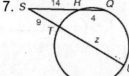

$z =$ _____

$SQ =$ _____

$SU =$ _____

8.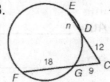

$n =$ _____

$CE =$ _____

$CF =$ _____

For each figure, determine the value of the variable and the indicated length by applying the Secant-Tangent Product Theorem.

9.

$x =$ _____

$IK =$ _____

10.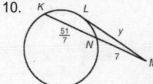

$y =$ _____

$KM =$ _____

LESSON
24-4

Segment Relationships in Circles

Practice and Problem Solving: C

For each figure, determine the value of *x*. Write your answers in simplest radical form if necessary.

1.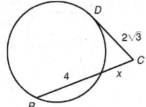

   x = _____

2.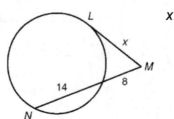

   x = _____

3.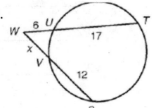

   x = _____

4.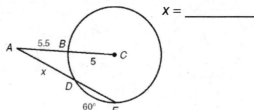

   x = _____

5.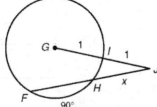

   x = _____

6.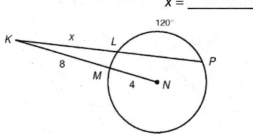

   x = _____

For each figure, determine the indicated length.

7.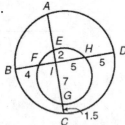

   AC = _____

   BD = _____

8.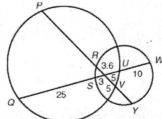

   PY = _____

LESSON 24-5

Angle Relationships in Circles

Practice and Problem Solving: A/B

For each figure, determine the measure of the angle by applying the Intersecting Chords Angle Measure Theorem.

1.   m∠RPS = _____

2. 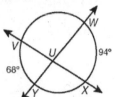   m∠YUV = _____

For each figure, determine the measures of the indicated angle and arc by applying the Tangent-Secant Interior Angle Measure Theorem.

3. 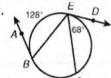   m∠ABE = _____

m$\widehat{CE}$ = _____

4. 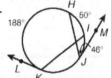   m∠LKI = _____

m$\widehat{IJ}$ = _____

For each figure, determine the value of *x* by applying the Tangent-Secant Exterior Angle Measure Theorem.

5. 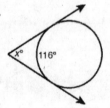   x = _____

6. 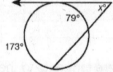   x = _____

7. 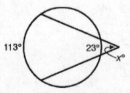   x = _____

8.   x = _____

For each figure, determine the measure of the intercepted minor arc.

9. 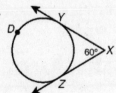   m$\widehat{YZ}$ = _____

10.   m$\widehat{DE}$ = _____

Name _____ Date _____ Class_____

Angle Relationships in Circles
Practice and Problem Solving: C

For each figure, determine the indicated angle and arc measures.

1.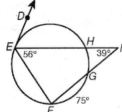

    m∠DEI = _____

    m $\widehat{EF}$ = _____

2.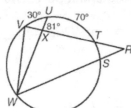

    m∠WVR = _____

    m $\widehat{TUW}$ = _____

Write paragraph proofs for Problems 3 and 4.

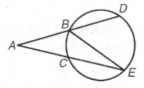

3. **Given:** $\overline{AB} \cong \overline{EB}$

    Prove: $m\widehat{DE} = 2m\widehat{BC}$

    _____

    _____

    _____

    _____

    _____

    _____

4. **Given:** $\overline{JK}$ and $\overline{JM}$ are tangents to the circle.

    Prove: $m\widehat{KM} < 180°$

    (*Hint:* Use an indirect proof and consider two cases.)

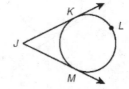

    _____

    _____

    _____

    _____

    _____

    _____

LESSON
25-1

Justifying Circumference and Area of a Circle
Practice and Problem Solving: A/B

For each figure, calculate the indicated circumference or area.
Give your answers in terms of π.

1.

   the circumference of ⊙V

   _____

2.

   the circumference of ⊙H

   _____

3.

   the area of ⊙M

   _____

4.

   the area of ⊙H

   _____

For Problems 5 and 6, determine the indicated measures.

5. What is the radius of a circle with a circumference of 2π centimeters? _____

6. What is the diameter of a circle with an area of 16π square meters? _____

Stella wants to cover a tabletop with nickels, dimes, or quarters.
She decides to find which coin would cost the least to use.

7. Stella measures the diameters of a nickel, a dime, and a quarter. They
   are 21.2 mm, 17.8 mm, and 24.5 mm, respectively. Find the areas of
   each coin. Round to the nearest tenth.

   _____

8. Divide each coin's value in cents by the coin's area. Round to nearest
   hundredth.

   _____

9. Which coin has the least value per unit of area? _____

LESSON 25-1

Justifying Circumference and Area of a Circle

Practice and Problem Solving: C

To estimate the circumference and area of a circle with a radius of 2 inches, cut out a square with side lengths of 4 inches. Place the circle in the square and cut diagonally at 45° angles at the corners as shown. The result is an octagon.

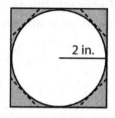

1. Find the perimeter of the octagon to estimate the circumference of the circle. Round to the nearest tenth.

   _____

2. Find the area of the octagon to estimate the circumference of the circle. Round to the nearest tenth.

   _____

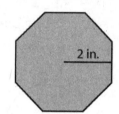

3. Use the formulas for circumference and area to find the actual circumference and area. Round to the nearest tenth. How do your answers compare?

   _____

4. Observe that the octagon is regular and circumscribes the circle. Using θ and *r*, as shown in the figure, write a formula for the perimeter of the octagon. (*Hint*: Use trigonometric ratios.)

   _____

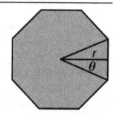

5. Next, write a formula for the area.   _____

6. Write general formulas for the perimeter and area of an *n*-gon that

   circumscribes a circle with the radius *r*. For *n*-gons, $\theta = \dfrac{360°}{2n} = \dfrac{180°}{n}$.

   _____

   _____

7. How do your formulas compare with formulas for the perimeter and the area of inscribed regular polygons?

   _____

   _____

LESSON 25-2

Arc Length and Radian Measure

Practice and Problem Solving: A/B

For each figure, calculate the length of the arc. Give your answer in terms of π and rounded to the nearest hundredth.

1.

   $\widehat{LM}$ _____

2.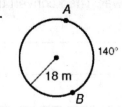

   $\widehat{AB}$ _____

3.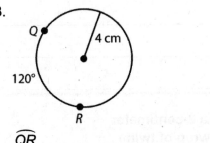

   $\widehat{QR}$ _____

4.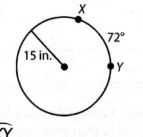

   $\widehat{XY}$ _____

5. What is the length of an arc with a measure of 45°

   in circle with a diameter of 4 miles? _____

6. What is the length of an arc with a measure of

   120° in a circle with a diameter of 30 millimeters? _____

7. The minute hand on an analog clock is 6 inches long.
   How far does the tip of the minute hand travel as time
   goes from 6:35 to 6:45? Round to the nearest tenth. _____

8. The minute hand on an analog clock is 8 inches long.
   How far does the tip of the minute hand travel as time
   goes from 1:27 to 1:43? Round to the nearest tenth. _____

Change the given angle measure from degrees to radians.

9. 10° _____

10. 225° _____

11. 144° _____

12. 50° _____

LESSON 25-2

Arc Length and Radian Measure

Practice and Problem Solving: C

1. Find the measure of the central of an arc so that the length of the arc is equal to the radius of the circle. Round to the nearest tenth. Explain your answer. Then convert the angle into radians.

_____

_____

_____

_____

_____

_____

Angela is wrapping 1 meter of twine around a spool with a 2-centimeter diameter. The spool is thin and accommodates only one wrap of twine before the twine stacks on top of itself. The twine has a diameter of $\frac{1}{2}$ centimeter.

2. Find how many complete times Angela will wrap the twine around the spool.

_____

3. Find the percentage of a complete circle that the last wrapping of the twine will make. Round to the nearest tenth.

_____

4. $\overline{AB}$ and $\overline{AD}$ are tangents to $\odot C$. Find the perimeter of the figure. Show your work.

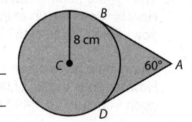

_____

_____

_____

_____

_____

_____

Name _____ Date _____ Class_____

Sector Area

Practice and Problem Solving: A/B

For each figure, calculate the area of the sector. Give your answers in terms of π and rounded to the nearest hundredth.

1.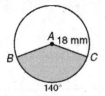

    sector *BAC* _____

2.

    sector *UTV* _____

3.

    sector *KJL* _____

4.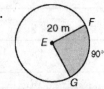

    sector *FEG* _____

5. The speedometer needle in Ignacio's car is 2 inches long.
   The needle sweeps out a 130° sector during acceleration
   from 0 to 60 miles per hour. What is the area of the sector?
   Round to the nearest hundredth.   _____

For each figure, calculate the area of the shaded region rounded to the nearest hundredth.

6.

    _____

7.

    _____

8.

    _____

9.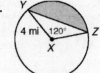

    _____

LESSON
25-3
Sector Area
Practice and Problem Solving: C

1. Find the measure of a central angle in a circle so that the segment has half the area of the sector. First derive an equation, and then use trial and error to estimate the measure of the central angle to within 1 degree. Explain your answer.

_____

_____

_____

_____

_____

_____

2. The circumference of a circle is 18π meters. Find the central

   angle of a sector of the circle whose area is 40.5π m². _____

For each figure, calculate the area of the shaded region rounded to the nearest hundredth.

3.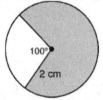

_____

4.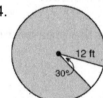

_____

5.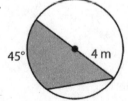

_____

6.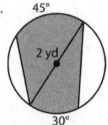

_____

Equation of a Circle

Practice and Problem Solving: A/B

Write the equation of each circle.

1. Circle *X* centered at the origin with radius 10   _____

2. Circle *R* with center *R*(–1, 8) and radius 5   _____

3. Circle *P* with center *P*(–5, –5) and radius $2\sqrt{5}$ _____

4. Circle *O* centered at the origin that passes
   through (9, –2)   _____

5. Circle *B* with center *B*(0, –2) that passes
   through (–6, 0)   _____

Graph each equation.

6. $x^2 + y^2 = 25$

7. $(x + 2)^2 + (y - 1)^2 = 4$

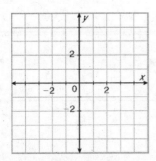

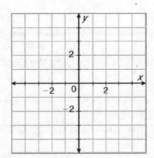

8. $x^2 + (y + 3)^2 = 1$

9. $(x - 1)^2 + (y - 1)^2 = 16$

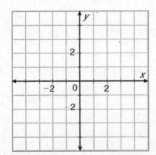

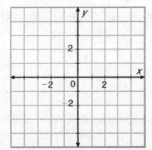

**Crater Lake in Oregon is a roughly circular lake. The lake basin
formed about 7000 years ago when the top of a volcano exploded
in an immense explosion. Hillman Peak, Garfield Peak, and Cloudcap
are three mountain peaks on the rim of the lake. The peaks are
located in a coordinate plane at *H*(–4, 1), *G*(–2, –3), and *C*(5, –2).**

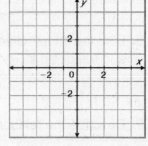

10. Find the coordinates of the center of the lake.

    _____

11. Each unit of the coordinate plane represents $\dfrac{3}{5}$ mile.

    Find the diameter of the lake.   _____

LESSON 26-1

Equation of a Circle

Practice and Problem Solving: C

1. Points A, B, and C lie on the circumference of a circle. AB is twice the radius of the circle. Find m$\angle ACB$.

   _____

2. Points A, B, and C lie on the circumference of a circle. The center of the circle lies in the exterior of $\triangle ABC$. Classify $\triangle ABC$ by its angles.

   _____

Give answers in simplest radical form if necessary.

3. The points $X(3, 4)$ and $Y(9, 1)$ lie on the circumference of a circle. There is exactly 60° of arc between X and Y. Find the radius of the circle.

   _____

4. Find the coordinates of all possible centers of the circle in Exercise 3.

   _____

5. Find the intersection point(s) of the circle $(x + 2)^2 + y^2 = 25$ and the line $2x + y = 3$.

   _____

6. Find the intersection point(s) of the circle $(x + 2)^2 + y^2 = 25$ and the line $y = \dfrac{4}{3}x - \dfrac{17}{3}$.

   _____

7. Describe the relationship between the circle and the line in Exercise 6.

   _____

   _____

8. Find the intersection point(s) of the circle $(x + 2)^2 + y^2 = 25$ and the circle $x^2 + y^2 = 9$.

   _____

9. Describe the relationship between the two circles in Exercise 8.

   _____

   _____

LESSON
26-2

Equation of a Parabola

Practice and Problem Solving: A/B

For Problems 1–2, state whether the statement is true or false.

1. The distance from any point on a parabola to the focus of the parabola is equal to the distance from that point on the parabola to the directrix of the parabola.

   _____

2. In parabolas that open downward, the focus is above the directrix.

   _____

For Problems 3–4, write the equation of the parabola with the given focus and directrix.

3. Focus: (0, 1); Directrix: $y = -1$

   Equation: _____

4. Focus: (0, –2); Directrix: $y = 2$

   Equation: _____

For Problems 5–6, write the equation of the parabola given the focus, directrix, and value of *p*. Then graph the parabola.

5. Focus: (6, –2); Directrix: $y = -6$

   $p = 2$

   Equation: _____

6. Focus: (–1, 2); Directrix: $y = -4$

   $p = 3$

   Equation: _____

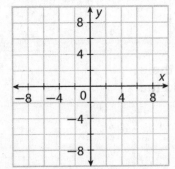

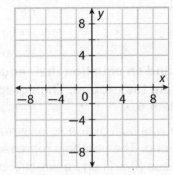

**LESSON
26-2**

Equation of a Parabola
Practice and Problem Solving: C

For Problems 1–2, write the equation of the parabola with the given focus and directrix.

1. Focus: (0, –8); Directrix: $y = 8$

   Equation: _____

2. Focus: (0, –2); Directrix: $y = 2$

   Equation: _____

For Problems 3–4, write the equation of the parabola given the focus, directrix, and value of *p*. Then graph the parabola.

3. Focus: (5, 7); Directrix: $y = 1$

   $p = 3$

   Equation: _____

4. Focus: (4, –3); Directrix: $x = -2$

   $p = 3$

   Equation: _____

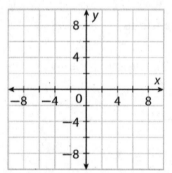 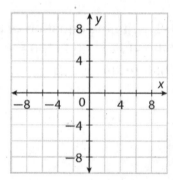

For Problem 5, find an equation that models the shape, using the *x*-axis to represent the ground. Then graph the parabola to find the answer to Problem 6.

A wooden bridge was built over a small stream. The bridge is 14 feet long. The parabola representing this shape has focus (0, –1) and a directrix of $y = 7$.

5. Equation: _____

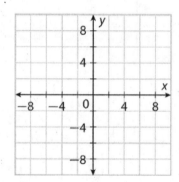

6. Which point on the shape identified the top of the bridge? What are the coordinates of this point? How tall is the bridge?

   _____